Speed Reading Secrets

The Backpack Study Series

Backpack Study Secrets
Backpack Speed-Reading Secrets
Backpack Term Paper Secrets
Backpack Test-Taking Secrets

Speed Reading Secrets

Read faster, remember more, and get great grades

Steven Frank

Adams Media Corporation
HOLBROOK, MASSACHUSETTS

Published by
Adams Media Corporation
260 Center Street, Holbrook, MA 02343

ISBN: 1-58062-025-6

Printed in Canada.

J I H G F E D C B

Library of Congress Cataloging-in-Publication Data
Frank, Steven.
Speed-reading secrets / Steven Frank.
    p.   cm. — (Backpack study series)
        ISBN 1-58062-025-6
1. Reading (Higher education) — United States. 2. Study skills — United States.
    I. Title. II. Series: Frank, Steven, Backpack study series.
        LB2395.3.F73   1998
        428.4'071'1— dc21   98-16310
                                                CIP

This publication is designed to provide accurate and authoritative information with regard
to the subject matter covered. It is sold with the understanding that the publisher is not
engaged in rendering legal, accounting, or other professional advice. If legal advice or
other expert assistance is required, the services of a competent professional person should
be sought.
    — From a *Declaration of Principles* jointly adopted by a Committee of the American
            Bar Association and a Committee of Publishers and Associations

This book is available at quantity discounts for bulk purchases.
For information, call 1-800-872-5627 (in Massachusetts, 781-767-8100).

Visit our home page at http://www.adamsmedia.com

Contents

Introduction

Are You One of These Students?

Highlighter Helen

Helen buys highlighters by the truckload. When she sets about her required reading assignment for class, she sits with her hot pink highlighter in hand, brandishing it like a machete above the page. As she reads, she highlights anything that sounds important, anything that is worth remembering, anything she might be tested on, and anything that confuses her. When her mind starts to wander, she doesn't really worry; as long as something is highlighted, she thinks she has "covered" it. When she's done reading, more of the page is now hot pink than white. Helen is satisfied with her work, certain that she's read the chapter thoroughly. So she is quite surprised when she does poorly on the final exam. And that's not the worst of it. When she tries to sell back her fifty-dollar textbook at the end of the semester, the bookstore won't take it. As the clerk tells her, "Who wants to buy a hot pink textbook?"

Bored Beth

Beth sits down to read an article entitled, "Semiology and Structuralist Criticism." "Yuck," she thinks, "this sounds totally boring." She reads the first few sentences and comes across terms she's never seen before, like "signifier" and "syntax," and begins to roll her eyes. "This is soooo boring," she whines to herself. She reads another line, then glances out the window. She stares for a while at the sky, the trees, the grass, and a cute dog catching a Frisbee, then goes back to her article. She's forgotten what she's read, so she has to start reading the article from the beginning. Rubbing her aching head, she reads the first two paragraphs, and soon finds herself thinking about her weekend plans. What will she do Saturday night? Who will she go out with? She forces herself to go back to her reading, but once again has lost her place. She starts the first sentence again, then decides the reading is just too boring and probably won't be on the test anyway. Unfortunately, she's wrong.

Crammin' Darren

Darren decides to get his reading done in one shot. He leaves Sundays open to be devoted entirely to doing all of his reading for the upcoming week. After he manages to wake up and eat breakfast, he locks himself in his room with his stack of books and articles. He proceeds to read each one, from beginning to end, and immediately move on to the next one. After the third hour or so of this, he notices his eyesight beginning to get foggy, his back starts to hurt, and he can't move his neck. He forces himself to keep reading, plowing through one book after another until he falls asleep at his desk. The next day, as if he had a bad hangover, he can barely move, has a splitting headache, and can't seem to remember anything he read the day before. It's all just a blur.

Reading Is Hard Work

As a student, much of your time will of course be spent in classes. But when you're not in class, you'll likely spend long hours hitting the books, and in many ways, this work is the most difficult. Reading textbooks and other required sources is a major part of the educational process, yet many students go about their reading in completely the wrong way, much like the readers above. We all think we can read fairly well; after all, most of us have been doing it since elementary school. But when it comes to serious academic texts, reading is much more difficult than the other kinds of reading to which we are accustomed. It requires a whole new set of skills and techniques.

There are several reasons why the reading you have to do for school is going to be more difficult than what you are used to.

Reading Overload

When you add up the amount of required reading for each week, you'll probably find it will take hours and hours to complete, more than seems humanly possible. You could try and read everything you are assigned, but you'll wind up spending most of your week doing it. You won't have much time to relax or socialize. You also probably won't be reading very efficiently; you won't really understand everything you read, and the reading ultimately won't help you on exams.

The fact is you don't have to read everything you are assigned. Professors generally assign far more reading than is absolutely necessary; they'll assign entire chapters or articles when only certain sections might be relevant. You also don't need to devote extensive time and concern to each and every assignment. Some kinds of texts you'll find relatively easy to read quickly; others — those that are more complex or contain more extensive and relevant information — you'll want to devote more time to. Later in this book, we'll talk about ways to prioritize your reading list for each week. You'll also learn ways to speed up your overall reading rate.

Poorly Written Texts

If you're having trouble understanding a certain source, particularly a textbook, you may be tempted to think it's your fault. You probably believe that a source as authoritative as a textbook has to be good, especially if it was assigned by a professor. There are indeed many very well-written textbooks that are truly informative and clearly organized. But there are also many poorly written textbooks, sloppily thrown together, that give students more headaches than helpful information. Don't assume that everything your teacher gives you is going to be expertly written, not to mention factually correct. Very often, teachers assign readings from textbooks as a kind of backup, to make certain that if a topic or issue isn't adequately covered in class, the students will have a chance to make up for it in their reading at home. The professor may not even have read the assignment herself! You're the one who is going to have to try to make sense of it. You can learn to be a critic of required sources, evaluating just how reliable and helpful they really are. If a source is poorly written, you can toss it and still do well in class.

Difficult Texts

As you advance in your education, you'll find that the kind of reading you are required to do is much more complex than you've encountered before. It's partly because you'll be coming up against more sophisticated vocabulary and terms, but it will also be due to the style in which academic materials are written. Academic sources are written in a particular way that is distinct from the everyday writing you see in a magazine or best-selling novel. People in academia are accustomed to this style; they're quite comfortable reading, writing, and speaking this way. But it's going to be new for you. Like learning a new language, it will take you time to pick up "academese" and feel comfortable reading it. You'll have to struggle with some of the texts you encounter, working very hard just to make sense of them. That's not necessarily a bad thing; struggling with a difficult text can be exciting and helps make the reading process more interesting. Best of all, the feeling that you've finally "got it" is extremely gratifying.

The main problem with these kinds of difficult texts is not the way they're written; it's the "boredom" excuse. When students encounter a difficult text, many are quick to dismiss it as boring rather than take the time to work with the text and try to understand it. Don't fall into the "boring" trap. When you sit down with a difficult text, be prepared to fight a bit — and reap the rewards when you're finished.

Pressure to Retain Information

When you read for pleasure, it's okay to forget the details, even the entire plot. However, when it comes to reading assignments for school, you'll be expected to do more than just read. You're going to have to *learn* from the reading and *retain* what you learn. Those readings aren't assigned for no purpose; chances are your teacher will expect you to remember what you've read and be able to use it. You might need the information for class discussion. You might be tested on it. And that puts extra pressure on you while you read. You can't just sit back and enjoy; you need to work to absorb and retain the information. Without some kind of strategy or technique to help you do so, reading can become an even more intimidating, difficult chore.

The Wandering Mind

When it comes to reading for classes, the most common problem students face isn't tough vocabulary or work overload; it's the way their minds just seem to wander all over the place, more interested in everything *other* than the assignment. There are all kinds of distractions to keep your eye and your mind from the page; don't underestimate how powerful they can be! Many distractions come from the surroundings — noises, music, other people in the room, the telephone. Just as many, though, come from within your head. You'll be reading along and suddenly your thoughts will turn to something completely differ- ent — a conversation you had earlier in the day, your plans for later, your shopping list, your favorite episode of *The Brady Bunch*.

Just about anything can pop into your head when you should be focusing all your attention on reading. And once you are distracted, it's all the more difficult to get on track. You might have to start from the beginning of the chapter, which makes the total time spent reading much longer than it needs to be. Or, you might just keep reading without even realizing how much you've missed while you were thinking about things like television reruns and what's for dinner.

Don't feel bad if your mind tends to wander when you have to read for a class. You're not alone, and it's under- standable. It's not easy to concentrate on required read- ings, especially if the topics don't interest you or they are poorly written. But there is hope.

So What's the Answer?

Did you ever read a book that you just couldn't put down? A murder mystery? A trashy romance? You become so involved in the plot that your mind never once wanders. Why should it be different reading textbooks and other required assignments? The difference is that when you pick up a real page-turner, you have a vested interest in what you are reading that keeps you engaged. Very simply, you want to find out what will happen. Who is the killer? Will he murder the heroine? Will the main couple wind up together, or lose one another forever? That interest in the material keeps you so deeply involved in what you are reading that you don't want to turn away even for a second.

This book presents a way to read that helps spark the same kind of involvement with your textbooks and other required readings as you experience with a page-turner. Of course, you're not likely to find a textbook you just can't put down; but you *can* learn ways to become much more interested in and engaged with whatever you read.

We think that when we sit down and open a book and read, we will somehow absorb all of it. In actuality, you can read every word on the page and not understand a bit of it. In order to become an *effective* reader, you have to be an *active* reader. That means doing more than just looking at the words on the page; it means becoming involved with the material and *thinking* while you read.

This book outlines strategies to help you become a more active reader for all of your reading assignments. By being an active, thinking reader, you'll not only get reading done, but retain what you read. That means you'll be better prepared to understand future reading assignments and participate in class; best of all, it means you'll be much better prepared to take exams for which you are expected to apply what you've read all year.

The first half of this book concentrates on reading to learn; in other words, reading in such a way that you understand, learn from, and remember what you've read. We'll talk about the differences between types of reading materials, which pose a variety of challenges to you as a reader. And we'll look at a step-by-step strategy for any reading that will ensure you think about and learn from what you read. We'll also pay special attention to the tough texts that at first seem nearly impossible to follow. Using special techniques outlined later in the book, you'll be able to translate those tough texts into a language you can understand.

As a student, learning, understanding, and retaining information from what you read is your priority. At the same time, though, you're going to have an awful lot to read. So, in addition to learning how to read carefully, you'll also need to learn ways to read quickly. In the second half of the book, we'll look at strategies for how to handle your reading load while you're in school. You'll be happy to know there are several ways you can make your reading manageable — from reading selectively, to skimming, to speed-reading.

What, Where, and When to Read

What to Read

For most classes you take, there will be required readings you will be expected to keep up with throughout the term. The types of reading materials you'll read as a student fall into these general categories:

Textbooks. These large, bulky books encompass a tremendous amount of information about a particular subject. Textbooks are generally used in larger lecture classes in which the readings correspond to or supplement the material the professor goes over in class.

Articles and Essays. You may be assigned articles from newspapers or magazines, or essays from anthologies. These readings concentrate on a single particular subject, and they can range significantly in terms of difficulty. An article from a popular magazine is going to be much easier to read than one from a special journal for professionals in the field. Sometimes a professor might put together a special course packet that includes various articles for you to read throughout the semester; the professor might also hand out articles in class.

Works of Literature.   These are readings primarily in English classes, consisting of novels, plays, and poems. While some literature might be compiled in a textbook or anthology, most will be available as trade books you can purchase.

Other Primary Sources.   In addition to works of literature, there are many other original writings you might be assigned to read. These sources might be historical documents and speeches, philosophical essays and discussions, or reports on laboratory experiments. Unlike textbooks and articles, which might refer to or analyze these primary sources, these reading assignments enable you to encounter the original material for yourself.

Tracking Down Reading Materials

You should find out what the required readings are during the first week of classes and track down as many as possible. The readings should be listed on the course syllabus. If they are not, you can ask the professor if there are any required books you need to find for the course. The more you can find and get a hold of in advance, the less you'll have to worry about — and the less time you'll waste — once the school semester is in progress. If you have all the books on hand, each time you need to do a reading assignment you can get the book and begin, without having to first wander around trying to find the text.

If you can afford it, it's a good idea to purchase required books and study materials (like course reading packets); that way, you'll have them readily available and can make any notes you like in them while you read. If your college has its own bookstore, the books should be available there. When you go to the store, be sure you have all the information about the course with you — the course title and number, and the name of the professor. Find the course on the shelf (you can ask a clerk for help). Make certain the books you are purchasing are the same as those listed on your course syllabus. Sometimes the store can make a mistake and order the wrong titles.

If you know in advance what courses you are taking, you might want to go to the bookstore before classes start and buy some of the books. That way you can avoid the crowds that will be there at the start of the semester. There is a slight risk in doing this in that the teacher may, at some point, decide to change the required readings. If you purchase a book that is not being used for your course, see if the bookstore will let you return it.

Save Yourself Some Bucks: Book Bargains

Buying textbooks and other reading materials for classes can be a costly venture. There are, however, a number of ways to save some money.

> Buy as many required reading materials as you can in advance. If you can't buy a source, know what is required and where you can find it easily.

Buy Used Textbooks. Your school bookstore will usually sell several used copies of books required for your course, especially if they are popular books that are often used in different classes. The drawback to buying used textbooks is that they will often be marked up by previous students. Try to get to the bookstore early in the semester so you can sort through the pile of books and choose one that is relatively clean. Should you purchase a book that has notes or highlighted sections, try to ignore them as you read. Just because some other student felt these sections were relevant doesn't mean they will be to you.

Check Used Bookstores. Even if your school bookstore doesn't have any used copies of books you need, you can try checking local bookstores that specialize in used books. These stores will occasionally carry used textbooks, but you are more likely to find sources other than textbooks, such as novels, plays, and other primary sources. Either way, it's worth going to see what they have available in the store. Again, make certain you go early in the semester, as other students might have the same idea.

Borrow Books from Friends. Many people take the same or similar courses while in school. You can ask around and see if anyone you know owns the books you need and then try to borrow or even purchase the books from your friends. There is a chance, though, that your friend has an older edition of the book you need; just be aware of this as you read it. If possible, consult a current edition of the book and note any changes. You can skim the current edition in the bookstore, or ask someone in your class if you can borrow his or hers for a few hours.

Share Books.   Some students who are friends and enrolled in the same class consider chipping in for the books and sharing them. This does save money but is not recommended, as sharing books can cause more problems than it's worth. Since you both need access to the books, each person has less time available to read and study them. This is particularly a problem preceding major exams, when you are both going to want to consult the book for an extended period of time. However, if you are really trying to save money, you can consider this as an option. You'll just need to work harder to organize a tight schedule in which you have enough access to the books.

Go to the Library.   The school library will probably carry many of the sources that your teacher requires for your class. If you can use a library book, you are obviously going to save a great deal of money. However, there are certain drawbacks to depending on library books. You may need a certain book throughout the semester, but you will only be able to check it out from the library for a few weeks.

Moreover, other students — even those who are not in your class — will also want those books, and the library will have limited copies, so there's no guarantee you'll get the books when you need them. If a required book for your class is going to be used repeatedly, then you should probably not rely on using a library copy. However, if it is a book that will only be used for a week or two (such as a novel you are reading for an English class), then you might consider trying to get the book out from the library.

If the book is located in the reference section of the library, as many textbooks probably would be, then you don't have to worry. You just need to be willing to sit with the book in the library and take notes. Many professors also put the books required for their courses on reserve, which means the books cannot leave the library and students are given a limited amount of time to read them. If books are on reserve, you know you'll be able to get a hold of them at some point. Ask the professor if the books are on reserve; if they are not, you can suggest that the professor place them on reserve for you. Try to start reserve reading well in advance of the due date. That way you don't need to worry if you get to the library and find someone else has the book, or find you need several sittings to complete the reading.

Selling Back Books. At most school bookstores, you can sell your books back at the end of the semester to receive a partial refund. Consider saving whatever money you get to use toward books for the next term.

Keep in mind, however, that the cleaner your copy is, the more money you will get back. If the book is heavily marked up, the bookstore may refuse to buy it back at all. If you are planning to sell your books, then, avoid using highlighters or taking notes in the book. That shouldn't be a problem; if you follow the reading and note-taking strategy outlined in this book, you won't need to highlight or write in the book at all.

Many students think that as long as they highlight sections of a chapter, they've read it. In reality, highlighting a passage only means that they've looked at it. They haven't necessarily thought about it and absorbed what they've read. When it comes time to study for exams, they then have to go back and reread all those highlighted sections. That takes a whole lot of time that could be spent studying. You'll be glad to know that the reading strategy outlined in this book doesn't require that you write in or mark up the textbook at all. Believe it or not, you'll read much more efficiently and be better prepared for exams than if you did highlight. If you do want to write in the textbook, though, do it in pencil. That way, you can erase it at the end of the semester and still get money back.

Where to Read

Many study guides insist that the only way you can read is holed up at some cubicle in the library, sitting on a hard-backed chair. While that will certainly minimize outside distractions, it won't necessarily make you a better reader. You are going to spend many hours reading each semester, so you may as well read somewhere that you feel comfortable. Of course, you don't want to be so comfortable that you fall asleep. But if you are serious about your work and actually complete assignments, there's no reason you can't read in your room or even in bed.

No matter where you read, you do need to minimize the outside distractions, or move someplace where you will not be bothered. If you can't ignore a phone call, consider turning off the ringer and disconnecting your answering machine. If you can't help but look outside and daydream, close the drapes, or choose a spot away from a window. If your friends, family, or roommates keep interrupting you while you are studying in your room, find someplace else to work. By the same token, studying in the library won't help you if friends keep coming over asking how you are doing and what you thought of last night's episode of *ER*. Find an isolated spot in the library where there won't be many people walking by.

No matter where you decide to study, make certain it is well-lit. You're going to be reading a great deal while you are in school and it does take a toll on the eyes. If a room isn't well-lit, you'll find yourself straining to see and getting headaches. Sometimes areas of the library can be dimmer than your desk at home.

It's okay to listen to music while you read, at home or in the library (as long as it's on a portable headset). Listening to music can drown out many of the outside noises that can distract you. However, you should be careful about the kind of music you choose. You want to have music on that will be in

> Choose a place to read that is well-lit, comfortable, and free from frequent distractions. If you find you are not reading productively, change your location, or take extra measures to minimize distractions.

the background, rather than attract your attention. Something old, that you are very familiar with and that makes you feel comfortable and relaxed, will probably be better than something you just bought. Keep the music on lower than you would normally listen to it. It will be on in the background and relax you, but it won't necessarily occupy all your attention.

You might find it helpful to decide on one specific location where you always go to do your reading assignments — such as the library, your desk, your bed, a lounge. This can help make reading more of a comfortable habit. You know that as soon as you sit in this particular spot, it is time to do a particular activity.

However, you might also find it helpful to choose several different locations where you like to work, and move from one to another for a change of scene. A simple change of location can help you feel revived and ready to do more work, cutting down on some of the tedium. You might even consider designating different locations for different types of readings. For example, it makes the most sense to read a difficult textbook in the library, where there are plenty of reference books you can turn to for help as you read, while you can read plays and novels for English class lying on your bed. Do whatever works the best for you.

There is no right or wrong place to read as long as you feel comfortable *and* make progress. In any setting in which you study, do what you need to do in order to minimize outside distractions. Make a promise to yourself that if you are not in fact getting work done, you'll make a change and seek out a new place to work.

No Time to Nap: Staying Awake While You Read

It might sound like a joke, but falling asleep while reading is a problem that plagues many students. The need to sleep is powerful — and to fight it, you need to take equally strong measures. Here are a few important suggestions.

Get Enough Sleep at Night.   There's a simple reason why so many students fall asleep while reading, and it's not necessarily boredom. They're just tired. Of course, it's difficult when you are a student to get a good night's sleep all the time, and you shouldn't expect to. However, don't make a habit of staying up late all the time. Try as often as possible to get six to eight hours of sleep a night.

Don't Get Too Much Sleep.   You might not realize it, but there is such a thing as *too much sleep*. For most people, six to eight hours of sleep a night is sufficient. If you get more sleep than your body needs, you can feel sleepy all day long.

Exercise Regularly.   If you exercise regularly, you'll sleep better at night and be more energized during the day. That means you'll be more focused on your classes and your reading.

Become Alarmed.   If you tend to fall asleep while reading, set an alarm. You can purchase an inexpensive travel clock or wristwatch equipped with an alarm and have it nearby while you work. The alarm should be loud enough to wake you up but quiet enough not to disturb those around you. If possible, set the alarm to go off every fifteen minutes. If you can't set it to go off regularly, set it for a specific time (such as a half-hour after you've begun studying) and continue to reset it each time it goes off.

Arrange Wake-Up Calls or Visits.   If you don't trust an alarm, have a friend check on you every so often. The easiest method is to arrange to work together; that way you can keep an eye on each other and keep each other awake. Of course, you have to be careful that you both don't fall asleep at the same time, and also that you don't spend too much time chatting. If you are reading in your room, you can have a friend or relative give you a phone call every hour or so to check up on you.

Take Breathers.   If you become too comfortable while reading, it's easy to fall asleep. You should plan to get up and walk around at regular intervals — preferably outside. While fresh air can do wonders for waking you up, limit your walks to just five minutes. When you return to work, you'll feel revived and better able to focus.

Stay Actively Involved.   The more engaged in the material you are, the less likely you'll succumb to sleep. Rather than just reading the words on the page, have a conversation with yourself in your mind about what you read; read a few lines and then comment on them. We'll discuss active reading in more detail later on in this book.

Don't Get Too Comfortable.   It's important to be comfortable while you work because the more relaxed you are, the more open your mind will be. Additionally, being comfortable makes studying less tedious. However, there is such a thing as being *too* comfortable. If you find yourself constantly falling asleep, you should change your study habits. For example, if you study on a couch or bed, you might need to sit at a desk, where it is more difficult to fall asleep. If you listen to music, you might need to change your selection to something that will keep you up rather than lull you to sleep. Remember, read in an atmosphere you feel relaxed in, but not so much that you cannot stay awake.

When to Read

Each week, you'll likely have a number of required reading assignments you are expected to complete before coming to class. In order to devote enough time to complete all of the readings, you'll have to plan your schedule carefully. Time management strategies and special tips are covered extensively in *Study Secrets*, another book in the Backpack Study Series. In general, though, you can figure out times when it is best for you to read by following the suggestions offered here.

Schedule time to devote to reading assignments each week. Allow more time than it will likely take you to complete the reading.

Each week of each semester, there will be times when you are absolutely unavailable to do your schoolwork, such as when you are in class or are committed to an extracurricular activity. You can plot these times out on a weekly study schedule. This will enable you to see the hours you have available to work on assignments and read texts.

Next, you can make a list of the required reading assignments (and other study tasks) you have for the week and estimate the amount of time you think it will take you to complete each assignment. The amount of time you'll need to devote to reading will vary significantly from text to text, assignment to assignment. Often you can assume that longer assignments will take more time than shorter ones, but this is not always the case. A short but difficult text might take more time and effort than a long but simple article. As you'll see later in this book, different kinds of readings require different skills from you as a reader. Some readers find certain kinds of texts much easier to read than others.

In time, you'll gain a sense of how much time it will take you to read and take notes on different kinds of texts. In general, though, you should always estimate more time than you actually think will be necessary. That way you guarantee you can complete the work without feeling pressure to cram it into too brief a time period.

After you estimate the amount of time each reading will take, you can look at your schedule and find those "free" time periods in the week when you can devote enough time to doing the reading. Fill in the reading periods on your schedule for that week.

The time of day or day of the week you choose to read is a personal decision. In general, though, you should consider the following factors:

Leave Extra Time.   When scheduling time for reading, try to do it at times when you do not have a class or another commitment immediately afterward. That way, you are safe if your reading takes longer than you estimated; more importantly, you won't feel pressure while reading to get it all done by a specific time.

Spread Assignments Out.   Don't schedule one reading assignment right after the other, especially readings from different courses and subjects. Give yourself a break in between to take a breather. If you cram too many readings into a single time period, especially from different classes, you risk it all becoming intermingled mush in your mind. You might even consider devoting different days of the week to reading different subjects. Whatever you do, do not plan to do all of your reading for an entire week on one day — that's overloading yourself way too much, and it won't really be productive.

Sample Schedule for Reading Times

	Mon.	Tues.	Wed.	Thurs.	Fri.	Sat.	Sun.
9-10:00		English		English			
10-11:00	Psych 101	Read Chapter 9 for Soc.	Psych 101	Huck Finn, Chs. 11–15.	Psych 101	Finish Huck Finn	Read Ch. 10 for Soc.
11-12:00							
12-1:00							Read Articles for Psych. from Psych. Today
1-2:00	Sociology		Sociology		Sociology		
2-3:00		Biology		Biology			
3-4:00	History	Read Civil War Letters for History	History	Read Psych Journal Article	History		
4-5:00							
5-6:00	Gym		Gym		Gym		Gym
6-7:00							
7-8:00	Literary Magazine	Read Psych Text Chapter 8	Literary Magazine	Read Course Packet Article for Soc.			Read Hist. Articles and Ch. 2
8-9:00	Bio Text Reading Chapter 4		Read Lab Reports for Bio				
9-10:00				Chapter 1 of Hist. Book			
10-11:00	Huck Finn Chapters 1 & 2	Huck Finn Chapters 3–10					

= "Free" time

> Spread out reading assignments throughout the week. Do not do all of your reading at once. Try to give yourself a break between assignments, especially from different courses.

Getting — and Staying — Motivated

Even if you carefully schedule time for all your reading assignments, there is no guarantee you will *want* to do the work at those times. No matter how interested you are in the text, reading is still work. And sometimes, when it comes time to do work, you need to give yourself an extra kick in the pants. You have to motivate yourself to do work even if you don't feel like working; otherwise, you risk falling behind. And, when you have even more work to do piling up and feel pressure to catch up, you'll feel even less motivated to read.

One way to help yourself get motivated is to reward yourself when you accomplish specific reading assignments. As we just noted, when you estimate a period of time in which to read, you may finish earlier than you expected. Any time left when you've completed that assignment can be your personal free time. This in itself serves as a reward to get you motivated to read. For example, if you know you want to watch television at night, you can force yourself to read efficiently during the day. Similarly, if you want to go to a party on the weekend, you'll try your hardest to get all your reading done during the week. You just need to

To get motivated, promise yourself little rewards — like
a snack or a walk — for each task you accomplish.

remind yourself of the fun activities waiting for you when
you are finished working.

However, even with the promise of free time as a
reward, you may still find it difficult to get motivated
and begin reading. You can provide yourself with additional rewards as you work. Set small goals, and reward
yourself each time you fulfill them. For example, if you
have several hours blocked off on Tuesday night for
reading forty pages, promise yourself a snack after
you've gotten halfway through the assignment. This will
at least get you started.

These rewards don't need to be extravagant. A reward
can simply be a short break to do something you like —
getting ice cream, talking on the phone, going for a walk,
listening to music, whatever. Just make certain the
"reward" time is a short break lasting no more than fifteen
to twenty minutes.

This reward system is particularly helpful if you have to
spend long hours reading a tough text. If you think of
yourself as slaving away for many long hours, it will be
extremely difficult to motivate yourself to begin work.
However, if you divide the task into several smaller ones —
such as every chapter or every few pages — and promise
yourself a small reward at the completion of each one, it

will be much easier to get started. You know then that when you sit down to work, a reward of some kind is not all that far away.

SPECIAL TIP:
The More You Read, the Better You'll Read

Try making it a habit to read more frequently during your free time. Read newspapers, magazines, fiction, or nonfiction. Just by reading frequently, you become more accomplished at it. You will also learn all kinds of miscellaneous facts that you might be able to use in your studies at some point. Even a trashy novel might have something to teach you: A courtroom thriller could teach you something about the law; a romance novel set in a country you've never visited might teach you about foreign customs. Of course, you might not learn anything monumental; but even small things can be useful or simply interesting.

Reading for fun can also help you improve your vocabulary. Almost any time you sit down to read, you'll probably encounter some new word. Try to look up one new word that you've never heard before each time, and you'll steadily build your vocabulary.

Reading to Learn: Textbooks

*T*his chapter outlines a strategy for smarter, more effective reading of academic materials that will help you become a more *active* reader. By reading actively, you'll better understand and learn from what you read. You'll also retain more, thereby becoming better able to use the information you've read in class discussion and on tests, and apply the material to other readings and classes.

In the detailed description of the reading strategy steps that follows, we'll primarily be discussing ways to read textbooks. Many courses you take will have a textbook that has been written for that subject, especially in the survey and introductory courses you take in high school or as a college freshman and sophomore. This reading strategy can also be adapted for other sources, which we'll describe in the next chapter.

Getting Started

As you'll soon see, the reading strategy outlined in this chapter involves taking notes while you read. You might, therefore, want to read at a desk or table so you can keep paper handy and write as you read. If you're not at a table, have some kind of flat surface nearby (a large hardcover book or lap desk) on which to write.

You'll of course need paper to take notes on; the best paper for this purpose is loose-leaf paper. You can take notes and do other writing exercises on these loose sheets of paper, and then put them in three-ring binders or folders for safe-keeping. It's a good idea to keep a separate folder or binder for each class. That way you can keep your notes neatly organized and easily accessible for when you need them.

Make certain you write the date and author or title of the material you are reading at the top of each page of notes you take. That way if the sheets get out of order, you can easily put them back.

Active Reading: A Step-by-Step Strategy

1. Know Where You're Headed — and Why

When you go on a trip, you usually have a destination in mind and a route planned before you go. You know exactly where you are going and why — and that's what keeps you from getting lost. The same holds true for reading. If you don't want your mind to wander, make sure you know right from the beginning where you're headed and the route you are taking.

Before you begin reading, think a bit about *what* you are reading. What is the title of the chapter, article, or text? Does it give you any hint as to what you can expect to read? As with classroom lectures, each chapter or article you read will have a main topic. Make certain you know the topic before you start to read.

Next, try to get a sense of the chapter's contents. Glance through the chapter and look at the various headings and subheadings of different sections. Look at the pictures, diagrams, and charts. Try to get a sense of what topics are included within a chapter, how they relate to one another, and how they come together within the main topic.

As you embark on your reading assignment, you'll find that keeping the "big picture" in mind will help keep you on track. As you read, you'll have a sense of how each section fits into the overall text. You'll also know how much more material you have ahead of you, which can help you plan your time. As we'll also see, gaining a sense of the chapter's contents in advance can help you read more selectively.

In addition to getting a sense of what you are reading, try to keep in mind *why* you are reading. Of course, one reason you are reading this is because it is required by your teacher. But if that is the only reason, you are going to get bored with it pretty quickly. Each thing you read should somehow contribute to your understanding of the course material as well as your general knowledge. If you can designate a purpose for each thing you read, you'll feel better about doing the work. You won't be reading just to please the professor, but because you see some value in fulfilling the assignment.

Think about some of these questions:

- What do you think your professor is hoping you will gain by reading this?
- What might you personally gain from reading this?
- How does the chapter or text fit in with the overall subject matter of the course?
- How does the chapter or text fit in with the current topics of the course (i.e., the lectures for that week)?
- Does the chapter build on previous material from the course? How?
- Does the chapter prepare you for upcoming topics? How?
- Is anything in the chapter familiar to you (either from the course or from other classes and personal experiences)? What? Where and when did you first learn about this? What did you learn already? What in the chapter is new to you?

If you like, you can take a few minutes to jot down some notes on what you discover during this initial preview of the reading assignment. But even just thinking about these questions will help you become actively involved in the reading assignment right from the start. Contemplating these issues helps you evaluate how important the assignment is to you, which will also help you be a selective reader. These questions also help you gain a more personal interest in the reading by connecting it with your overall knowledge. That way, you won't feel you are reading just because it's required, but because it can somehow enhance your understanding of the subject matter.

Know where you're headed and why. Flip through and preview a reading assignment to get a sense of the big picture. This will help you stay on track while you read.

2. Take Brief Notes While You Read

Most students know how important it is to take notes during classroom lectures and discussions; few, though, realize how important it is to do the same while reading outside of class. Like your classroom lectures, the required reading assignments include important information you'll need to use later on. You might, for example, be expected to participate in class discussion or be tested on the material on exams.

You probably won't have the time to reread every assignment right before an exam — and even if you did, doing so much reading all at once would be a headache; it would certainly be tough to understand, absorb, and remember heaps of reading materials ingested all at once. However, taking some notes while you read the first time around provides you with an accessible, brief summary that can help you recall the assignment in more detail when you need to do so.

More importantly, taking notes while you read is one key way to make reading a more active and interesting process. You'll have something to do while you read, which will help you remain engaged with and receptive to the material. And when you're done, you'll have already absorbed and retained much of what you've read, simply by doing some of these active reading techniques.

But what should you take notes on? You're obviously not going to rewrite everything that's already in the book. What, then, is most important for you to write down? And just how should you do it? Here are some tips for note taking from reading assignments:

List Key Terms, Concepts, and Topics. As in classroom lectures, many reading assignments, especially in textbooks, are designed to convey important new information about a particular subject. Much of that information centers on *key terms*, such as names of important people or places, significant dates, and terms that refer to crucial theories, formulas, and facts. Most often, these terms are going to be new to you, which makes them harder to remember. A goal of note taking while reading, then, is to keep track of all these key terms.

In addition to key terms, you can also list all the major concepts, topics, and points the reading covers. For example, a chapter on the nervous system might include sections on the brain, the neurons, and electrical impulses. You can list these topics in your notes and then refer to them later on as a kind of index of the chapter. Very often, just reading a list of topics from a reading assignment is enough to help you remember the chapter in detail. If not, you can always go back to the chapter and read those sections you don't remember. You'll save time, though, as you won't have to read the whole chapter again.

Important key terms and many significant concepts and topics will be easy to spot in many readings — especially textbooks — because they'll be in bold or italics. You should pay

Don't worry about neatness or grammar; these notes are for your own benefit; as long as they make sense and are legible to you, they are fine.

special attention to these terms and be certain to write them down. Terms that are repeated are probably important too; repetition indicates the reading somehow concentrates a great deal on issues and ideas relating to those terms.

A bonus to noting key terms as you read is that there's a strong chance these terms and topics will also come up during classroom lectures or discussions. Keeping up with required reading can help a great deal when you take notes in class as you will feel somewhat familiar with the material in advance.

Include Brief Definitions and Explanations in Shorthand. In addition to listing the key terms and topics, you should also try whenever possible to write *brief* explanations or definitions of the term. Again, don't rewrite everything already covered in detail in the reading assignment. Try to jot down just a few words or phrases that will help you later on to remember what a term means as well as the major ideas covered in a particular reading.

Taking these notes should not take a great deal of time. The note taking is meant to supplement the reading assignment; if you spend too much time on it, you won't have time for other school work, and reading will become too much of a chore. You should be able to jot down these terms and definitions while you are reading. Keep your eye on the book, but a pen in your hand poised above the paper.

There are other ways in which you can learn how to take brief yet understandable notes as you read:

Avoid Complete Sentences.   There's no reason why your notes have to be written in complete, grammatically correct sentences. Sentences are filled with words that aren't necessary for one to understand the gist of them. You can still understand the basic meaning of a sentence without using all the words in it. For example, you can leave out articles (*the, a, an*) and pronouns (*he, she, they, it*) and still understand the basic information.

Keep Descriptions and Examples Brief.   Textbooks and other readings might include long passages as a means of illustrating or explaining some point. You don't necessarily need to replicate all of this in your notes. You can instead use a few key words to sum up the example or explanation. Those few words will usually be enough to trigger your memory of the entire account. If not, you can always go back to the original reading and reread the explanation yourself.

Abbreviate Repeated Key Terms.   Using abbreviations is an excellent way to take notes more quickly. If you can reduce words to just a letter or two, it is obviously going to help you write faster. But be very careful. When you abbreviate too many terms, your notes become difficult to read. And if your notes don't make sense to you, then writing more quickly didn't really help you. You should therefore only abbreviate key terms that are repeated frequently throughout the reading.

The best way to abbreviate is to use capital letters that stand for entire words. Usually you can just use the first letter (or few letters) of a word as its abbreviated form. For example, *Freud* in notes could be abbreviated as F. *Gross National Product* could be abbreviated as GNP.

You can also abbreviate words by leaving out vowels. For example, the word *group* can be abbreviated as *grp*.

It's a good idea to circle any abbreviations you use, so you'll recognize them. The first time you come across an important term, write out the entire term and circle it. This will serve as a signal that you will be abbreviating this term from now on. Then, each time that term comes up, use the abbreviation and circle it. If you don't want to circle abbreviations, you can indicate they are abbreviations by following them with a period.

In addition to using capital letters and initials, you can also abbreviate longer words by making them shorter. If a word or name has several syllables, you can use just the first syllable or two instead of writing out the entire word. For example, the term *autobiography* can be abbreviated *autobio*.

Signs and Symbols. It can also make note taking much easier if you use signs and symbols for certain commonly repeated words. But keep it simple. Don't fill up your notes with so many signs that they become impossible to read. Settle on a few common signs that you understand and use all the time. That way, when you read over your notes, you'll know what the signs mean right away without having to think about them.

Here are some suggestions for common symbols to help with your note taking. You can use these or come up with your own.

$+$	in addition, and
$=$	equals, is the same thing, is defined as
$\neq$	is not the same thing, is different, unequal
ie	for example
$\approx$	approximately
$\nearrow$	increases
$\searrow$	decreases
$\leadsto$	has an affect or influence on
$\longrightarrow$	leads to, results in
@	at or about
$*$ or !	this is an important point
VS.	compared to
— —	indicates a new point being raised
;	indicates a closely related point
( )	indicates additional information or a description of a point
(?)	I'm confused about this and need to double-check it

Construct a Rough Outline.   As you list key notes and concepts, you can place them into a rough outline that indicates how they are related to one another. Certain terms and concepts are closely related to specific topics, and these topics might in turn be related to even larger topics. Taking notes in outline form enables you to indicate on the page the relationships between those terms, topics, and concepts. Again, this will help you understand and retain the information from the chapter.

Don't get stressed out at the idea of making an outline. You may be thinking that outlines are real headaches, that they are overly complicated and don't help all that much. The reason you feel that way is probably because you've been taught that there's only one way to make an outline and that it's a complex matter, with Roman numerals and letters. You don't have to worry about any of that. When we talk about making a rough outline for your notes, we are talking about a simple diagram that helps you to keep track of how various topics, terms, and concepts are related.

You'll find that making an outline for a reading assignment is even easier than taking notes during a classroom lecture. Most textbooks, unlike certain professors, make it very clear how they are organized.

Generally, a reading assignment such as a chapter from a textbook will focus on a *main topic*. Almost always, that topic will be made obvious to you as the chapter will have its own title that indicates the subject. Sometimes the chapter will also be preceded by a brief description of the topic and contents. If not, your previewing for a sense of the big picture should have given you an idea of the main topic of the reading.

Within that main topic, the chapter will usually address various additional topics that provide more detailed information about or fall under the heading of the main topic. Within those topics, there might also be several subtopics that more specifically relate to those topics, and so on. The key terms and concepts you are listing will generally fit into one of these areas.

Again, the various topics and subtopics will often be easy to spot in a textbook as they will be listed as subheadings above the passages of text that discuss them in detail. The subheadings might be in a different typeface, or in boldface or italics, or they might be centered above the text. The passages underneath those headings will include the key terms and concepts that relate to those topics. Many books will even list (either in the contents or at the start of the chapter beneath the title) the topics covered in that particular chapter.

Most books other than textbooks will also differentiate between the more important topics and the lesser important ones by changing the style and size of the typeface of the headings. For example, the more important headings might be larger and/or in boldface, while lesser important ones will be smaller and in lighter or italic type.

As you read, you can watch out for headings and subheadings in a chapter. As they come up, write them down on the loose-leaf paper (either writing them as they appear in the text, or writing a few words that will help you remember the topic as it appeared). Beneath those headings, you can then list the key terms and concepts that are raised in that section of the reading.

Jot down brief notes while you read. Keep a list, if possible in outline form, of the key terms and topics that are covered in the text. You can also include brief explanations, definitions, and descriptions.

As with any outline, the less important a topic is, the more you indent it on your paper. Don't worry about including Roman numerals or letters. You can simply skip lines between topics, and indent terms beneath the blank lines to show that those terms are part of the topic.

Here is how a rough outline, without any Roman numerals or letters, might look for a typical chapter:

MAIN TOPIC OF THE CHAPTER
(centered and underlined at top)

TOPIC A (The first topic the chapter raises)
(with lists of key terms and concepts related to this first topic with brief definitions)
    — Subtopic of Topic A (with lists of key terms and definitions)
    — Another Subtopic of Topic A (with lists of key terms and definitions)

TOPIC B (The next topic the chapter raises)
(with lists of key terms and concepts related to this next topic with brief definitions)

— *Subtopic of Topic B (with lists of key terms and definitions)*

— *Another Subtopic of Topic B (with lists of key terms and definitions)*

3. Write a Response

When they get to the last sentence of a reading assignment, most students think, "Whew! That's finished. What a relief!" and close the book without giving it another thought. They don't realize that a great deal of the work they've just done will have been a waste of time. While they have read the assignment, they have not really *thought* about it. They looked at the words on the page, but they haven't thought about what they mean. They don't know if they even understood what they just read. In short, they haven't really learned anything based on what they've read.

If you want to learn something from what you read, it is crucial that you *think* about it after you've finished reading. An excellent way to keep you thinking about what you've read is to write a reading response.

To write a reading response, you simply write whatever you want to about what you've read.

First, close the book and put it aside, and take out a few sheets of fresh paper. Draw a line down the page so that you have an extra-wide left-hand margin of about three inches. Your paper should look like this:

Write your response only on the right side of the margin; you'll use the space on the left-hand side later on. Set a time period during which you will write about the assignment without stopping. You can set a limit of about five or ten minutes per assignment. Or you might set a page limit of one or two pages of response for every five you read. It's up to you how you do this; just make certain you always write some kind of response.

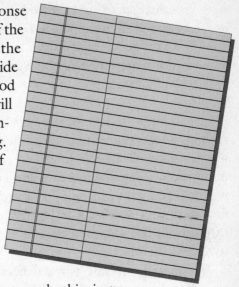

Then start writing.

First and foremost, you can take a few moments to consider and jot down the chapter's general themes. To help you identify these themes, you might want to think back on what you've read and consider these questions:

- What seemed to be the author's main concerns in this chapter?
- What ideas, topics, or points were mentioned more than once?

- Was there any kind of introduction or conclusion in the chapter? If so, what points did the author make here?
- Did you get a sense of the author's opinion or stance on the material he or she was addressing in the chapter? What was it?

In addition to helping you recall the overall content of a reading assignment, these notes on the themes of the reading assignment will enable you to compare the key themes of all the reading assignments and classroom lectures. This will help you gain a sense of how various parts of the course fit together. And it's a safe bet that when themes show up throughout the semester, they're important concepts likely to appear on an exam.

A reading response is *not* necessarily a summary of the chapter, although you should, in part, note the major themes and topics covered. Instead, it's your opportunity to engage with the material you've just read. Think of yourself as having a conversation with the text, or perhaps with the author of the text. This is your chance to share whatever is on your mind in response to what this other person has just told you.

After noting the general themes, here are some other questions you might address in your response:

- What is your emotional reaction to what you've read? Did you like what you read? Why or why not? How did reading the text make you feel? How do you think the writer wants you to feel?

34

- What points do you think were most important to the writer? Did the writer successfully convey these points to you?
- What parts, if any, did you have trouble understanding? Why? What made it confusing?
- What questions about the text do you still have? In the response, you should list as many questions about the chapter as you can possibly think of. Make certain you list questions about any terms, topics, or points you didn't understand. You can also list questions you have that arise from what you have read. What additional questions about the subject matter do you have that were not addressed in the text? By the way, these questions don't necessarily have to be answered right away. They may be answered as you read more throughout the semester; or, they may never be answered. But either way, asking questions gets you thinking about what you read and makes you more responsive to the material.
- How does this text connect with other things you've learned? Does it tie into things you've studied in other courses? Does the reading remind you of anything else you have learned or experienced?

These are just some suggestions of topics you can address in your response. But you can feel free to write about anything you want, just as long as it is in direct response to the reading. This isn't a diary. You don't want to spend the time writing poems or making a shopping list. When you sit down to do the reading response, let yourself write down whatever comes into your head about the reading.

Even though you write the response *after* you finish reading, writing these responses is going to help you become a more effective reader; they will encourage you to be a more active participant in the reading process. Many students approach required readings like mindless robots; they focus on the words on the page and try to suppress any of their own thoughts or feelings about the chapter. But the mind wants to be more involved than that. And if it's not involved, it is going to wander.

You are not a robot. You are a real person who has thoughts, feelings, and opinions about what you read. You are allowed to like something you read, or to hate it. You are allowed to be confused or excited by things you read. The response gives you the opportunity to express all of these things you are thinking and feeling while you read. As you read, think about the things you want to say back to the author or the text that you will include in the response. Since you are allowing your mind to think more actively about the text, your mind won't be as likely to jump to other thoughts. It will have plenty to keep it interested and engaged in the text.

4. Follow Up

Before an exam, you can read through your notes and responses to help you prepare. As you study the notes, if you have difficulty remembering or understanding something, you can always return to the original text and reread that section.

When you're finished with the reading, write a response identifying major themes, and describe your overall reaction to the material. Imagine yourself having a conversation with the text.

In addition to using the notes for study before an exam, it is worth it to read the notes and responses regularly throughout the semester. If you can, you might even designate one day a week for reading the responses from the previous week's readings. Reading these responses can serve two important functions: helping you identify areas that confuse you in time to try to understand them better, and enabling you to make connections between various readings, class lectures, and discussions. As you read each response, jot down any new thoughts, ideas, and questions in the wide left-hand margin you left open.

You'll find that as a course progresses and you get deeper into the subject matter, you'll gain a better understanding of key concepts. You'll also start to see how different concepts are related to one another and how they fit into the "big picture" of the overall course. A reading assignment that initially confused you may make much more sense later in the semester. Long after you've completed a reading, you might begin to see how the material relates to another reading or topic covered in class. You can then go back over your initial response and make notes in the left-hand column that indicate what you now understand about the reading.

Additionally, as you read your response, look for any questions you might have had while reading the material. Make a note of this question or point of confusion in the space you left on the left-hand side of the page. Once you identify these questions, you can now make an effort to find answers and/or learn to understand what initially confused you.

Many students make the mistake of ignoring those sections of a reading that confused them, assuming they are not relevant or will not show up on a test. However, much of that information may in fact be extremely important. If you were confused by something in the original text, you can and should make an effort to understand it. But you don't have to do it all on your own. There are many places you can go to for help, if you're willing to make the effort.

You can start by tracking down and reading other books on the same topic. By reading someone else's explanation, you might begin to get a better understanding of the material. In general, the more explanations and interpretations you read, the more complete an understanding you gain.

Other textbooks are good places to find more information. You don't have to buy another textbook, although you may want to if it will be very helpful. Many school libraries have several textbooks in the reference section. You also need not limit your research to textbooks. Go to the library and look for other books on the subject. If you need suggestions for books and articles to examine, check your textbook to see if there is a bibliography (list of sources used in the book) or a list of suggested further reading.

You can also check the subject catalog at the library for other books on that topic. You don't necessarily have to go in search of a specific source; you can simply to go the section of the library where that particular subject is shelved and browse. You'll be amazed at the kinds of things you find. Very often you will get lucky and find a book that covers the course topics clearly and concisely. There may even be a study guide with beautifully written summaries of all the topics you're researching. As you browse, check the tables of contents and indexes for the terms you need help with. You can also go to bookstores with decent academic and scholarly sources, such as campus bookstores, and browse.

The Internet is another valuable resource for getting information. If you have access to the Internet and are comfortable using it, you might find all kinds of materials that can help increase your understanding. Use a search engine to find Web sites by subject.

Asking the professor for extra help might seem like the best way to get a quick and easy explanation of something that confuses you, but it isn't always. For one thing, there's no guarantee he will provide any better an explanation outside of class than he did inside of it. Another problem is that if you always rely on your professor for explanations, you give the impression that you cannot think for yourself. You don't want a professor to have that picture of you in mind when he assigns your grade.

If you are having real trouble understanding an important issue, however, feel free to go see the professor during office hours. In fact, going to see your professor a few times a semester is a good idea. That way the professor gets to know you by

Read over your response and write in any new thoughts or ideas in the left-hand margin. Look for any questions and points of confusion, and then get help. Seek out other sources of information, and take notes on what you find out.

name and you give the impression of being a student who cares about the subject and your education. Just don't overdo it.

As you get more information from these other sources, jot down more notes. You can use the left-hand column of your notes and responses to take notes from these other sources.

In the end, you should have a set of notes that accurately reflects the topics and terms covered in a reading assignment — and that you fully understand. Best of all, this entire process of preparing these notes and responses has made you actively involved in reading. Without even realizing it, you may have already retained large chunks of information from the text, without having to consciously study or memorize parts of it.

What to Do with the Notes When You're Done

After each reading assignment, when you're done taking notes and writing responses as described above, you should keep them in a binder or folder, preferably where you also keep your classroom notes.

If the reading assignments don't coordinate with the lectures, you might want to keep the reading notes in a separate section of your loose-leaf binder. But usually, your professor will coordinate reading assignments with lectures. If this is the case, then keep the reading notes alongside the lecture notes in the same binder at home. By keeping lecture and reading notes side by side, you'll be able to observe the ways in which the reading assignments and lectures fit together. For example, you'll see if certain points are covered repeatedly, an indication they are especially important and more likely to show up on an exam.

If your professor has assigned a reading for a particular day, you might want to bring your notes from your reading with you to the lecture so that you can refer to them as needed. For example, if the professor introduces a new term you recognize from your reading, you can quickly check your reading notes for the proper spelling. Additionally, you might be able to save time during the lecture. For example, if you know you've already defined a particular term in your reading notes, you won't have to do it in your lecture notes.

Just make certain you only bring notes to class that correspond to that day's reading assignment. Leave the rest at home in your binder so that you don't risk losing them.

Sample Textbook Chapter and Student Notes

Here is a sample passage from a textbook, along with the notes and response a student might write after completing the reading. If you like, you can treat this like an exercise. Read the following textbook passage, take your own notes, and write your own response. Then compare it to the notes and response that follow the excerpt.

CHAPTER 2
CLASSICAL THEATER
•••••••••••••••••••••••••••

In this chapter we cover:
- Ritual Origins of Theater
- Customs and Trends of Greek Theater
- The Development of Greek Tragedy
- Architecture of the Theater

THE ORIGIN OF TRAGEDY
Although exact accounts of the origins of theater in ancient Greece do not survive, many believe it evolved out of religious rituals. These rituals were primarily in honor of Dionysus, the Greek god of wine and fertility.

According to Aristotle's *Poetics*, the earliest account of the origins of Greek drama still in existence, tragedy grew out of *dithyrambs*, hymns sung and danced to honor Dionysus. Over time, dithyrambs became quite elaborate, involving entire choruses who sang and danced. Occasionally the chorus related stories and episodes derived from myth.

Although the exact manner in which the dithyramb developed into tragedy remains unclear, people speculate it was the result of an innovation made on the part of a member of the chorus who stepped out of the chorus and added additional lines, spoken as a character. Although there is no solid evidence to support this, the person credited with this innovation is *Thespis*, who, as a playwright himself, would go on to win the first dramatic contest presented in Athens.

DRAMATIC FESTIVALS
The Greeks paid homage to their gods at elaborate annual festivals. The primary ones were held in honor of Dionysus, including the City Dionysia, held in Athens. As far as we know, this was the first festival at which drama was presented and tragedy officially sanctioned. Playwrights presented several plays throughout the festival, and the winner was granted a prize.

DEVELOPMENT OF TRAGEDY
Tragedy is usually dated back to 534 B.C. when it was given official recognition as a part of the festival called the City Dionysia. Unfortunately, no drama from the sixth century survives. What we know about Greek tragedy comes

from the work that remains from the fifth century. All tragedies that survive from the fifth century are the works of three playwrights: Aeschylus, Sophocles, and Euripedes.

The oldest surviving plays are by Aeschylus, who is credited with the innovation of adding a second actor to the stage. Prior to Aeschylus, custom dictated that only one actor appear on stage, in addition to the members of the chorus and the choral leader. Sophocles, following Aeschylus' lead, introduced a third actor. The additions of these actors on stage enabled drama to become more complex. The playwrights were now able to depict open conflict between characters.

STRUCTURE OF CLASSICAL TRAGEDIES

Most Greek tragedies follow a similar overall structure. They begin with a *prologue* in which events that have taken place prior to the opening of the play are communicated to the audience. Following the prologue comes the parados, the highly ceremonial entrance of the chorus. The chorus usually has an opening speech in which their role in the play is introduced and they set the mood.

The chorus usually served a dual function. As times they chanted, sang songs, danced, told stories, and provided exposition. At others, though, they functioned as an actual character within the play, often engaging in dialogue with the other characters.

Following the parados, the rest of the play consists of a series of episodes divided by choral songs, known as stasima. At the conclusion of the play, the exodus is the final departure of all characters and the chorus from the stage.

THE THEATER ARCHITECTURE

As dramatic festivals became more popular, permanent theater spaces began to be constructed. One such theater was the Theater of Dionysus in Athens. The main feature of the theater was the orchestra, or "dancing place." It was a large open area where the action primarily took place. Originally, the audience sat or stood on a slope facing the orchestra. Eventually, the *theatron* was added. The theatron, which means "seeing place," was a series of permanent rows of benches, in circular fashion, that rose above the orchestra. The final component of the Greek theater was the skene, which means "hut." The skene was a small building set back from the orchestra. While it was often used as a dressing room, the structure itself often acted as a setting for the play. This is why many Greek tragedies are set in front of a palace or tomb.

Example of Notes on the Textbook Entry

CLASSICAL THEATER
The Origins of Tragedy
—Came from rituals to Dionysus = god of fertility, wine
—Aristotle's Poetics: trag. from dithyrambs = elaborate rites to D.
   —innovation by chorus leader, speaks in character
   —credited to Thespis

Festivals
—held in honor of D.
—City of Dionysia (CD) in Athens

Development of Tragedy
—534 B.C. = trag. officially recognized at CD
—6th c. = no remaining plays
—5th c. = 3 trag. playwrights
   —Aeschylus; adds actor 2
   —Sophocles; adds actor 3
   —Euripedes

Structure of Classical Tragedies
—prologue
—parados = chorus enters (role of chorus = sing, chant, also acts as character)
—episodes
—stasima (choral songs)
—exodus

The Theater
—Theater of Dionysus
—orchestra (dancing space)
—theatron (seeing place) = circular seats
—skene (hut) = dressing room/set in background

Example of a Reading Response to the Text, with Additional Follow-up Notes

READING RESPONSE: CLASSIC THEATER, CHAPTER 2

	I thought the chapter was dry; the information was just presented in a very straightforward way without much color. But I found that if I tried to imagine what theater was actually like in ancient Greece, it made the reading more interesting. It sounds like the theater of that period was really imaginative.
When we read about Japanese Noh theater, I again observed this connection between ritual and drama.	The author seems to emphasize the connections between religion and theater; he keeps showing how theater emerges from religious rituals. The orderly structure of the tragedies he describes did sound very ritual-like. I wonder what other aspects of Greek drama are similar to ritual. Today's theater is like a ritual as well—there's a definite order of events as well as a certain awe people feel for live theater. But I thought the Greek festivals sounded more like the Cannes film festival than religion. I'd like to get a better idea of what exactly went on during those festivals.

READING RESPONSE: CLASSIC THEATER, CHAPTER 2 (cont.)

In chapter 3, we read more on this. The addition of a second and third actor adds more conflict. It takes at least two people to have an argument, right?	I've heard of those three tragic playwrights before, but I don't know much about them. I remember reading Antigone in high school (which one wrote that? I think Sophocles). I know we're going to be reading more plays by these guys in class. I want to see exactly how they are different from each other. How much of a difference was made by adding that second and third actor?
We learned about Aristotle's theory of tragedy. Did Shakespeare follow this theory? I need to look into this.	The layout of the theater sounds cool. I tried to picture how it looked. It would be great to see a play in one of these theaters. They remind me a bit of what I heard about the Globe Theater where Shakespeare was first performed—people also sat in circles around the stage. I wonder if there are other similarities in the two theaters. Actually, I really wonder if Greek tragedy is similar to Shakespearean tragedy. The structure described in this chapter was certainly different from the structure of tragedies in Shakespeare.

Reading to Learn: Other Sources

*I*n the previous section, you learned about an active and effective reading strategy for reading textbooks. While many college and high school classes rely on textbooks, especially for introductory and survey courses, you will probably be assigned readings from a variety of other sources.

For these sources, you can generally follow the active reading strategy outlined and discussed in the previous chapter. However, you may need to emphasize certain steps more than others, depending on the type of source.

These are some of the typical sources you might encounter, with discussions of specific active reading strategies for each type:

Magazine and Newspaper Articles

Teachers often distribute articles from magazines or newspapers as additional required readings in a course. These articles can come from a variety of sources, from mass marketed popular publications, to professional and scholarly journals. They can also vary significantly in terms of length and difficulty.

For any article, make certain you first preview the material to get a sense of the big picture — what the article is about. This will also help you determine how much time and effort you need to devote to reading the article and writing your notes and response.

In general, articles concentrate extensively on a specific subject, explored in depth and in detail by the writer. Very often, much of an article will be devoted to communicating ideas and information, as in a textbook. You therefore do need to be on the lookout for key terms and topics, and take notes on them. The key terms and topics might be more difficult to spot, though, as articles will not necessarily highlight them with special typeface. Any term you see repeated often, or that seems to be important to the article's discussion, is worth writing down.

Key terms in articles might not be as clearly defined as in a textbook, which is geared toward students and usually clearly explains and defines any new information. As you take notes and write down key terms, try to indicate your sense of what a term means. If you do not know the exact definition of a key term, write it down with a question mark, and circle the question mark so you can spot it easily. Later on, when writing or following up your response, you can look up the term and write in its definition. Don't worry about the exact definition of the term, though, during your initial reading of the article. Looking up every term while you read can disrupt the flow of your reading.

In addition to noting key terms, try to list the various topics and subtopics introduced in the article. This listing will help you later on as you try to remember what was covered. If an article is divided into different sections with subheadings above them, those subheadings will often indicate new topics being introduced.

The style of an article might vary considerably. Many will be written in a journalistic, straightforward manner; the primary aim of such articles is imparting information (for example, about a person, place, phenomenon, or event), in which case taking notes on key terms and listing topics and concepts is your major concern. In other articles, though, a writer might be constructing some kind of argument, or extrapolating certain concepts in detail. In these cases, in addition to taking notes, you should write a detailed, extensive response, as this will enable you to engage fully with the ideas and opinions being expressed.

An important issue to consider in the response is how this article supplements the subject matter of your course. Why might your professor or teacher have assigned it? How does it connect with other reading assignments? With classroom lectures and discussions?

As you read, jot down notes, if necessary, on key terms and topics in rough outline form. Following the reading, write a response. Remember, take more time to write the response if the article addressed complex, sophisticated

> You can adapt the active reading strategy outlined in the last chapter to other sources besides textbooks. Some sources might require you still take extensive notes on key themes and topics. For others—such as works of literature and certain primary sources—you'll only need to jot down some notes to help you remember major points for discussion in your more detailed response.

concepts. Follow up later on, rereading your response, jotting down new thoughts and, if necessary, looking to other sources for more information.

Works of Literature

For many classes, primarily in departments of English, Theatre, and Comparative Literature, you will be required to read works of literature, such as novels, plays, and poems. Unlike reading assignments for other classes in which you read to learn about and retain new information, terms, facts, concepts, theories, and ideas, reading these works involves *interpretation*. As you read, you attempt to figure out what the works *mean*— the ideas, themes, issues, and philosophies that are being expressed through a creative and artistic use of language. It is important that you read these works carefully and thoughtfully — and before the due date in class. These works will often be the focus of lectures and classroom discussions; if you haven't read the material yet, you will be unable to understand and/or participate in the class.

As with anything you read, be certain to first get a sense of the big picture. Preview the material by looking carefully at and reading any information on the outside and inside cover. Glance through it and look at any introductory material, chapter or section headings, and pictures. Get a sense of how long the work is. Try to determine what this particular work has to do with the topics and themes of your class.

You can also think about what you already know about the writer and/or work, as this information can help your reading. For example, literary styles change in different time periods. If you know when a work was written, you might then have some idea of what to expect in terms of the issues, themes, and style of the work. Similarly, certain writers are known for creating certain kinds of works or dealing with the same issues and themes. If you know a bit about a writer's reputation and background, you can then have a sense of what to expect in the work you will be reading.

As you read works of literature, you really won't have to take notes on key terms and topics. (You will, though, still need to do that in readings for literature classes in which you learn new literary terms.) Don't worry, therefore, about taking notes as you read; concentrate instead on writing a very detailed reading response covering particularly the various issues listed on the following pages.

Although writing a response is your primary activity when reading literature, you might still want to jot a few notes as you read just to help you remember aspects of the reading to address in your response. You might, for example, like to list characters' names and relationships to one another, or list some of the events in a plot.

When you finish a particular reading, write your response immediately, while the text is fresh in your mind. Give yourself a good chunk of time to do this, as you should write a longer, more detailed response than you might for other kinds of assignments (fifteen to twenty minutes rather than five or ten).

For longer works of literature, such as novels and long plays, you probably will not be able to read the entire work in one sitting. In this case, you should write a response each time you read a portion of the text. Your response can address specifically whatever you have just read during that period. When you have finished the entire work, take some time to reread all of your responses and then write a final response in which you discuss the work as a whole.

In your response, try to address these particular issues related to literary interpretation:

Content/Plot

First and foremost, briefly address what is being discussed or described in a particular work. For novels and plays, you can briefly describe the plot, meaning the events that take place in the work. If you have only been assigned a portion of a larger text, such as a chapter of a novel or a scene from a play, you can describe the events of that particular section. When you finish the entire work, make certain to write a new response in which you describe the plot for the work as a whole.

In addressing the plot of a novel or play, you can also discuss the time period and setting in which it occurs. This information provides important background that often relates to specific details in the plot.

Some literary works, particularly many poems, do not have explicit plots in which things happen to characters. They still, though, will be aimed at describing or expressing *something*. Do your best to identify and describe the content of the work, even if it is not a plot. For example, the content of the *Ode to a Grecian Urn* is a detailed description of the scenes on a Greek urn.

Form/Genre/Style

In addition to observing *what* is being described or expressed, it is important to consider the *way* the writer chooses to express it. The terms *form*, *genre*, and *style* all relate to this element of literature. Form and genre are more technical terms. Form refers to the organization or structural principle for a work of literature. For example, the form of *Huckleberry Finn* is an autobiographical account, which has certain characteristic, identifiable elements. The form of the poem *Ode to Autumn*, is an ode, which similarly has distinctive elements.

Related to form, genre pertains to the type or category in which a literary work falls, such as comedy and tragedy. In your literature classes, you will probably discuss issues of form and genre and learn how to categorize works accordingly. If you understand genre and form, you can address this in your response.

However, if you are uncertain how to categorize in this manner, you can still discuss your overall sense of the work's style in your own words. An easy way to do this is to consider how realistic the writing is versus how the author may use artistic or experimental devices. Does the writing function according to standard, familiar rules of grammar? Does it attempt to replicate in writing the real world as we know and experience it? If not, in what ways is the writing doing something different? Is the difference an issue of the way in which language is used? The kinds of images that are depicted?

After describing in your words the style of a piece, try to determine the effect of that writing style. Writers choose to write in particular ways for a reason. Does the style in some way relate to what is being discussed? Does it create a particular emotional or intellectual response in you as a reader? If the same material had been written about in a different style, how would your reaction change?

Point of View

The point of view refers to who is doing the narrating, telling, or describing in a work of literature and the perspective they bring to bear. Different points of view include:

First Person. A character in the work narrates events referring to him or herself (using the term "I said," for example). Sometimes the first person narrator will be very much involved in the events of the plot; other times, he or she might merely be an observer.

Omniscient Narrator.   This refers to an unseen, unnamed, godlike narrator who does not participate in the plot but knows everything that occurs, including individual characters' thoughts and feelings.

Limited Third Person Narrator.   This point of view employs an unnamed, unseen narrator who is not a character in the story; however, unlike an omniscient narrator, this narrator has a limited perspective. He or she cannot see into characters' heads and describe their thoughts and feelings.

In some works, the point of view might even shift from section to section. At times, for example, an omniscient narrator may follow one character for long sections, and shift later to describing the perspective, feelings, and thoughts of a different character.

Tone

Refers to the attitude the narrator/author seems to have toward the characters and events in the novel. Examples of tone are: dramatic, humorous, sarcastic, ironic. The tone of a work can be quite difficult to determine, particularly in more complex or sophisticated works. For example, in certain satires, the narrator or characters might be tremendously serious about themselves, but the author tries to make them seem silly to the readers as a means of mocking them.

To try to determine the tone, look to your own feelings as you read. What reaction do you have to the material? Does it make you laugh? Are you afraid or upset? Do you think that is the author's intended response from you? What in the text particularly leads to that response? It can also be helpful if you know something about the particular writer you are currently reading. What kinds of work does he or she typically write?

Try to describe your sense of the tone in your responses. Don't worry if you are "right" or "wrong." As you have class discussions with fellow students and your professor, you will probably get a firmer grasp on the tone. Be certain to indicate any new thoughts on tone in subsequent responses or in follow-ups to earlier responses.

Images and Symbols

Try to briefly describe or even list any particularly vivid images or moments in the text. Very often, these images are utilized as symbols; they indicate a deeper and more significant idea than their surface appearances suggest. If you can, try to determine what the symbolism of a particular image is. Think about how that image connects with the plot and characters, as well as themes (see next section). Even if you cannot determine the symbolism of a particular object or image, it is still worth noting. You might at a later date come to understand what that image does in fact mean.

Themes

A work of literature's themes are the deeper, more significant ideas, concepts, arguments, and meanings that the work's content and form suggest. For example, some themes in *Romeo and Juliet* are: the impetuousness of youth, the power of love to overcome obstacles, the temptation of the forbidden, and how tragedy can lead to change.

A work can have any number of themes, and some may be more significant than others. Certain sections of a work might have their own individual themes, while the work as a whole has more major themes. The theme might be explicitly introduced in the text, perhaps in lines of dialogue or in the narration. It also might be implied by the events that take place. As you address all the other elements listed here in your response, ask yourself, "What does all of this mean?" "What is the big idea here this writer is trying to express?" Again, your understanding of the themes may change through subsequent readings and class discussions. Keep listing anything you think might be a theme.

Questions/Reaction

In addition to addressing the literary issues listed above, use the response to explore your personal reaction to what you've read. List any questions you have and describe how the work makes you feel, or what other topics and works it reminds you of. Very often, these gut responses do relate to issues of interpretation. How a work makes a reader feel and the questions it invites him or her to ask can be vital to the author's intention. At the same time, by writing a bit about your personal response, you remain an active reader. You might use some of these personal reactions and questions in class discussion to demonstrate your thoughtful participation in the class.

Special topics to address in responses to works of literature and many primary sources include: content/plot, style/form/genre, point of view, tone, imagery/symbols, themes, and questions.

Writing these responses will ensure you read actively and retain what you read; it will also help you begin the process of interpreting the material.

Don't worry as you write the response whether your interpretations are "right." For one thing, interpretation is very much subjective; different people can read and understand different works in different ways. However, interpretations do need to be based on facts as they appear in the text. By writing a response immediately after you read the piece, you have the text in mind and can specifically mention elements of it as you think about it.

You also don't need to worry whether or not you've figured out the entire text. You can use the response to begin sketching in your thoughts and reactions. Very often, you'll first read a work on your own and then have a class discussion about it. After you discuss the text in more detail in class, you will probably come to understand the text better and have a more accurate, thorough interpretation of it. If you are reading a longer work of literature, your understanding of it will also change over time as you read more of it. Once you finish a work, for example, you might realize that certain events or images that happen early on are much more significant.

SPECIAL TIP FOR READING LITERATURE

Consider purchasing a dictionary or glossary of literary terms to keep on hand. You can then look up and read more extensively about any literary terms you learn about from class discussion or that come up in your reading. You might even start by looking up the terms mentioned in this chapter, such as *genre*, *tone*, and *point of view*. As you become more familiar with these terms, you gain a more sophisticated vocabulary for discussing and interpreting works of literature. As you learn new terms, try to incorporate them into your reading responses. This will help you become more comfortable with using those terms, which can be valuable and impressive when writing papers, participating in class discussions, and taking exams.

As with your responses to other kinds of reading assignments, take the time at some point to reread your responses to works of literature and jot down any additional thoughts, ideas, or questions you have in the left-hand margin. Be sure to add new notes in the margins based on your subsequent readings and class discussions, as well.

Other Primary Sources (Nonfiction)

Textbooks and many articles are considered *secondary* sources, in that they utilize and discuss other writings and sources. Those sources, such as works of literature, are *primary* sources. In addition to works of literature, there are many other nonfiction primary sources you might be required to read. As with literature, it is usually extremely important that you read primary source materials that are assigned to you as they will often be an important element of class lecture and discussion.

As with anything you read, take the time to first look over the material and get a sense of the big picture. As part of this process, you might also consider the writer. Is the writer a well-known figure? What are she or he known for? Is she or he writing on something in their field? Is this work significant to their reputation? What do you already know, if anything, about the writer?

Some primary sources impart new information and include many key terms, much like textbooks or news articles. The key terms, though, may not be as easy to spot as in textbooks. As you read, you can jot down any term you see repeated often or think is significant to the text. Also try to include brief explanations.

Most primary sources won't center as much as textbooks do on key terms and topics; instead, they might be elaborations or meditations on some topic or theme, without much interest in introducing new terms and concepts. Rather than taking notes on key terms and making outlines of these sources, your primary concern should be writing a detailed reading response. As you read, you can if you like jot down any terms or phrases that will help you remember points to address in your response. But you don't necessarily need to take detailed notes. For these sources, you should devote more of your time to writing a detailed response than to taking notes.

After you read the piece, write a detailed response. As with textbooks, writing the response for these primary sources will provide you with notes to help with preparation of exams, help you pinpoint topics and concepts about which you have questions, and make you a more active respondent who has already thought extensively about and begun to retain material from the reading.

When writing responses to these primary sources, you can address the same topics as you do with works of literature: content, form, style, tone, point of view, images, themes, questions, and personal reaction. In your responses to nonfiction primary sources, noting the content and themes is going to be particularly crucial, as these documents usually address or explore some specific topic in detail. Make certain you can identify general themes and ask yourself questions about them.

At the same time, don't assume that just because these works are nonfiction that issues of style, form, and imagery are not relevant. While most primary sources won't necessarily have as experimental or artistic a use of style and form as works of literature, they are still written a particular way with a particular tone that could be relevant. All writers make choices in how they present ideas and make their points. These choices are known as rhetorical strategies.

As you note the general themes and topics addressed, it is worth it to notice the way in which they are being presented. Is there a connection between what is being addressed and the way it is being described? Why might the writer have chosen these particular strategies for making his or her points? What are the strengths and weaknesses of this style of presentation?

By considering and writing about these kinds of issues in your responses, you more closely examine the work, gaining a more accurate understanding of it. That, again, will help you retain information from it for later use.

Here are descriptions of some of the various kinds of primary sources you might be assigned, as well as specific questions and issues you should address in your responses to them:

Scientific Reports, Studies, and Experiments

One kind of primary source that you might read for many science and social science classes includes laboratory reports, accounts of experiments, and scientific studies. The most important element you read and make a note of is of course going to be the outcome of the experiment. But don't be fooled into thinking you only need to read the conclusion. You should make certain you have a sense of the general parameters of the experiment, such as the design of the study and who participated.

Also, try to evaluate the study: Are there any flaws in the design of the study or in the scientists' reasoning? Are there any factors that could have influenced the findings other than the ones the scientists discussed? What are the assumptions that were made in the study? Were the scientists aware of these assumptions? These issues often form the basis for examination questions. On the other hand, many lab reports will include lengthy sections in which the writers review relevant articles and studies that influence their own methodology. Unless your professor tells you otherwise, it is probably not as important that you read this section about other sources as it is for you to read about and understand the nature of this particular study.

Historical Documents

For historical documents, first note what event or events are being discussed. Another relevant issue is who the author is and from what point of view they are writing. Is the author an active participant in the events or an outside observer? Is she writing about events in her own time, or looking back at a previous time? What evidence does she use to support her depiction of events? Is her point of view at all biased? How is this bias evident or might it affect the discussion? Are alternative viewpoints expressed?

Essays and Commentaries

Essays that explore some subject or make a commentary on some event can be as artful and creative as works of fiction. In discussing essays and commentaries, you can use the same criteria as works of literature, observing not only the content and subject matter, but the way in which the writer expresses himself. How does the writer's style help him make his point or express his ideas? What is effective or ineffective about this style? What tone does the piece seem to be written in? Serious? Overly serious? Comic? Sarcastic? How does the tone fit with the subject matter?

> Always follow up: Look over reading responses and write in any new thoughts, ideas, or questions you have. Try to make connections between that text and others you read, or with topics raised in your classes. If you still have questions or are confused about certain points, turn to other sources for more information. Add to your notes and responses whatever you discover.

Philosophical/Theoretical Explorations.

You might be assigned certain readings that explore complex philosophical or theoretical questions, which may or may not be resolved. These works can be difficult in that they treat subjects in an abstract manner, talking about big, somewhat vague concepts without much use of specific detail. A good strategy for reading these works is to identify the overall question or questions that are identified and explored. Ask yourself what about this topic leads to this extensive questioning. What are the various viewpoints, ideas, or solutions to those questions that are proposed? What arguments or examples, if any, are given in support of the writer's explanation? What other views or opposing views examined? Are they refuted? How so?

Follow Up

Don't forget to follow up on your responses at some later point. Go back, read over your responses, and jot down any new thoughts or information you have since attained. You might come to know and understand much more about these primary sources after lectures, discussion, and more reading. See if you can tie the piece specifically to other works you've read, or other topics addressed in class. You can also turn to other sources to get new information about any questions or points of confusion you had after your first reading of the piece. You can add those notes in the left-hand margin of your response.

Remember the Big Picture

The reading assignments you do for your classes are not isolated exercises without any point. Each piece you read is a part of the bigger picture of that particular course or subject; it is also a part of an even bigger picture: your general knowledge. In fact, even the reading you do on your own time contributes something to your general knowledge. You learn *something* from *everything* you read, whether it be a textbook or a mystery novel or a magazine.

For each thing you read, whatever the type of source, keep the bigger picture in mind. Ask yourself what, exactly, you are learning from reading this piece? How is this text contributing something to your overall knowledge? As long as you keep that big picture in view, you'll always be an active and effective reader.

Grappling with Troublesome Texts

While many reading assignments will be fairly straightforward, you are probably going to encounter some that are tremendously difficult, presenting additional challenges to you as a reader and requiring special attention.

Academic writing can be difficult to read for several reasons:

1. The texts address more complicated ideas than other readings and are geared toward a more sophisticated audience. Unlike textbooks, which are usually written to present and clarify information to a student population, more complex academic texts are often written by professionals in the field for those they consider their peers.

2. As these texts are written for fellow academics, they include difficult vocabulary words and terms with which you as a student might be unfamiliar.

3. They also presume you already possess a fair amount of knowledge about a particular topic and are familiar with the key terms; if you do not know the terms, texts, theories, and concepts to which these articles refer, you immediately will feel at a disadvantage as you read.

4. Academic writing is often written in a style that uses long, complex sentence structures and paragraphs that can be difficult to follow all the way through.

To sum up, academic texts are difficult because they are written in a particular style featuring sophisticated language, complex sentence patterns, and intricate structural arrangements. This style can be very hard to understand, especially if you aren't used to it. In a way, learning to read this kind of writing is akin to learning a foreign language. That's good news, though, because anyone, if they are willing to put in the time and make the effort, can learn a new language. And the more you read of a foreign language, the better you can get at understanding it.

In the meantime, though, you can help yourself through difficult texts using a strategy similar to that used by students learning foreign languages: translation. Think of the entire exercise of reading these texts as translating the "academese" into a language you can understand.

What follows is a step-by-step strategy for working with and learning to understand complex, difficult texts.

Be willing to fight. Don't give up on difficult texts. Any work you do to try to understand them is better than nothing.

1. Put up a Fight

The most important rule for grappling with these texts is that you be willing to struggle with them. It's always easier to avoid a problem or a difficult situation by making excuses, but you don't gain anything that way. Don't give up reading a difficult text by making excuses like "this is boring" or "this is pointless" or "this is just too hard for me." Instead, go in fighting and put up a struggle.

Acknowledge that a text is difficult and therefore will take more effort than usual, but don't give up completely. Be willing to devote additional time to reading these texts and learning from them as much as you can. At the same time, take the attitude that even if you can grasp just a small portion of the text, it's better than nothing. You may even surprise yourself and pick up more than you thought you could. You'll also find that when you do master some or even all of the texts that initially seemed impossible to read, you'll feel a tremendous sense of satisfaction.

2. Read the Whole Text from Start to Finish

In the discussion of reading strategies earlier in this book, you read about the importance or previewing material to get a sense of the "big picture." When it comes to reading difficult texts, you should do more than merely glance through the text to gain this big picture. Instead, take the time to read through the entire text from beginning to end. For this first reading, don't worry about understanding everything you read. Don't bother yet to look up any new words or reread sections that confuse you. Just read it all, from start to finish.

Rather than trying to understand every word, line, and paragraph of the text, concentrate more on getting the gist of it. Even if parts of a text are totally incomprehensible, the main points may still be crystal clear by the time you get to the end. As you read, don't focus on each individual part; just be aware that they are pieces in a larger structure. Try to identify the themes of the text and keep them in mind as you read. If you come across difficult sections of the text, see if you can figure out how they tie in with the main topic.

When you are finished reading the entire text, ask yourself, "Okay, what did I actually understand or learn from this reading?" Take a few minutes to write down *anything* new you did learn, no matter how big or small it is. It may just be the names of a few important people, or it may be a whole new theory. When you're done, you'll see that even if you have not understood everything you just read, you did in fact learn a great deal — things you would never have learned if you had given up right at the start.

For very long texts, rather than reading the entire text all the way through, which can be very time-consuming, you can break it down into a few readings. For each one, write down what you did understand from reading that portion.

Sample Difficult Text and Student Notes

Below is a section from a difficult text. As a practice exercise, read the entire selection once and then write notes on anything you did learn or understand from the text. Then read the student's notes that follow.

> — *From* The Birth of Tragedy *by Friedrich Nietzsche*
>
> We shall have gained much for the science of aesthetics, once we perceive not merely by logical inference, but with the immediate certainty of vision, that the continuous development of art is bound up with the Apollonian and Dionysian duality — just as procreation depends on the duality of the sexes, involving perpetual strife with only periodically intervening reconciliations. The terms Dionysian and Apollonian we borrow from the Greeks, who disclose to the discerning mind the profound mysteries of their view of art, not to be sure, in concepts, but in the intensely clear figures of their gods. Through Apollo and Dionysus, the two art deities of the Greeks, we come to recognize that in the Greek

world there existed a tremendous opposition, in origin and aims, between the Apollonian art of sculpture, and the nonimagistic, Dionysian art of music.

These two different tendencies run parallel to each other, for the most part openly at variance; and they continually incite each other to new and more powerful births, which perpetuate an antagonism, only superficially reconciled by the common term "art"; till eventually, by a metaphysical miracle of the Hellenic "will," they appear coupled with each other, and through this coupling ultimately generate an equally Dionysian and Apollonian form of art — Attic tragedy.

Example of Student Notes after First Reading of Text

I know from the title that this has something to do with tragedy. The passage also has something to do with the Greeks, which I guess makes sense since I know that Greek tragedies are pretty famous. It is also about two different aspects of art that have something to do with the Greek gods Apollo and Dionysus. The Apollo side is related to sculpture, and the Dionysus side is related to music.

Read the entire text without worrying about what you do or don't "get." Write down everything you did understand.

3. Break Down and Translate

After that initial read-through of the text, you should now go back to the start and reread the text. This time, though, break it down into smaller chunks. Proceed to "translate" each chunk by reading the section carefully, looking up certain unfamiliar terms, and writing down in your own words a summary of that section, or at least what you do understand about that section. It's up to you how long each chunk is that you choose to examine in this manner; it can be a few sentences, an entire paragraph, or even a longer section of the text.

For each chunk of text, read slowly and carefully; if necessary, read it several times through. On a separate piece of paper, or in the margin of the text if there is room, write a "translation," noting entirely in your own words the general idea or the gist of that chunk. You do NOT have to write a word-for-word translation. Just indicate, to the best of your ability, what idea(s) that specific section of the text is conveying. If you only get a part of it, that's fine. Write down whatever you do in fact understand about that chunk.

> Break down and translate. Read the text again, reading one "chunk" at a time very carefully. Write down your sense of the "gist" of that chunk. If necessary, look up significant words and terms.

As you try to understand and write down the "gist" of each section, there still may be much you do not understand. If you like, you can write down next to that section, "I still don't get this part...." That's okay. As we noted earlier, the more you come to understand about a text, the better. It's more information than you had before beginning this careful reading process. And we're not done yet; there's still more helpful steps to come.

It's up to you to choose how much text to examine, and the time and effort you put into writing these "translations." It will depend partly on factors such as the time you have available for reading, and the length of the entire reading. To help save time, you can choose to translate only some portions of text — perhaps those that seem most important or most difficult. You can also look at and summarize longer chunks of text; rather than providing a summary of every few sentences, you might do so for every few paragraphs.

Just remember that everything you read carefully this way will teach you and help you understand something new — which is always going to be more productive than giving up on the whole reading.

Looking up Difficult or New Words

As you grapple with particularly troublesome texts, you are likely to encounter many words with which you are unfamiliar. You do not necessarily have to look up each word you do not understand. That's going to wind up taking a lot of time; it's also going to disrupt the flow of your reading and make it harder for you to keep track of the general themes of the text. Very often the context of a new word will be enough to help you get at least a partial sense of what a word means.

At the same time, certain words and terms will clearly be important, and in those cases, you should go ahead and look up the term. For example, if any word is repeated, then you might want to go ahead and look it up. Chances are this word is one commonly used in academic texts or in writings related to this particular subject; it is therefore probably worth knowing as you'll likely encounter it in the future. You might also find that a particular word, even if not repeated, is crucial to the entire meaning of a chunk of text. If that is the case, you also should probably look it up.

You can begin looking up words and terms in a good collegiate dictionary. It's well worth it to buy a dictionary and keep it on hand as you read. For certain kinds of readings, depending on the subject matter, you may like to have other sources on hand. For example, there are specialty encyclopedias and dictionaries for specific subjects (such as medical dictionaries and encyclopedias of literary terms) that include many more terms and more extensive information on each.

If you do take the time to look up a word, it is worth writing down its definition. (As you'll see in the next chapter, you can keep a log book for listing new words and their definitions). That way you can try to memorize it, or at least refer to it, if you encounter the word later on. You should also use the word when you write your "translations" of each text and include brief definitions of the terms. Using terms in your writing and conversation is one way to retain them for the future.

In addition to looking up certain words as you grapple with difficult texts, you should make the effort to improve your vocabulary in general. The more extensive your vocabulary is, the easier reading these difficult texts will become — and the more you'll understand. The next chapter outlines a strategy for improving your overall vocabulary.

Sample Breakdown and Translation of Difficult Text

Following is the passage from Nietzsche broken down into chunks with sample student "translations" after each. As an exercise, try to do your own translation of each chunk of text before reading the sample notes that follow.

(NOTE: You can choose to use longer chunks than those given for the purposes of this exercise — whatever helps you most in understanding the selection.)

We shall have gained much for the science of aesthetics, once we perceive not merely by logical inference, but with the immediate certainty of vision, that the continuous development of art is bound up with the Apollonian and Dionysian duality — just as procreation depends on the duality of the sexes, involving perpetual strife with only periodically intervening reconciliations.

> We'll understand more about the science of "aesthetics" (theories about beauty and art) when we understand that the development of art has to do with the "duality" (having a double nature) of the Apollonian and Dionysian. This is just like "procreation," (conceiving and then giving birth) which depends on two sexes, who sometimes conflict and sometimes come together in peace. I get this part, but I still wonder what Apollonian and Dionysian mean.

The terms Dionysian and Apollonian we borrow from the Greeks, who disclose to the discerning mind the profound mysteries of their view of art, not to be sure, in concepts, but in the intensely clear figures of their gods. Through Apollo and Dionysus, the two art deities of the Greeks, we come to recognize that in the Greek world there existed a tremendous opposition, in origin and aims, between the Apollonian art of sculpture, and the nonimagistic, Dionysian art of music.

The terms Dionysian and Apollonian come from the Greeks, whose view of art has to do more with their gods than with concepts, especially Apollo and Dionysus, two gods related to art. These gods to the Greeks had opposite purposes, A. tied to sculpture, and D. tied to music.

These two different tendencies run parallel to each other, for the most part openly at variance; and they continually incite each other to new and more powerful births, which perpetuate an antagonism, only superficially reconciled by the common term "art"; till eventually, by a metaphysical miracle of the Hellenic "will," they appear coupled with each other, and through this coupling ultimately generate an equally Dionysian and Apollonian form of art — Attic tragedy.

These two ideas about art, from A. and D., are parallel and lead to powerful births, but there is an "antagonism" (conflict) between them that is only partly reconciled by the term art. By some kind of miracle of the will, they couple, and produce "Attic tragedy" which is equal parts Dionysian and Apollonian. (I still don't get what Dionysian and Apollonian mean).

> Reread notes and write a response. Read over all of your notes so far. Then write a response, in which you make connections to other texts you've read, and note questions still remaining.

4. Reread Notes and Write a Response

After completing the "break down and translate" exercise, read through all of your "translations" that summarize the gist of the various chunks in the text. Then, write a response to the entire reading, just as you did for the reading strategies outlined in earlier chapters.

Set aside a specific amount of time to write the response. Be sure you leave an extra-wide left-hand margin for taking follow-up notes later. In your response, discuss what, if anything, you came to better understand after your initial read-through and "translation." You can also take this opportunity to address your personal response to the reading. Try to connect the text to others you have read, to other experiences you've had that you can relate to, or to subjects that came up in relation to the course. Most importantly, ask questions and note anything that troubles or confuses you.

On the following page is a sample response to the passage from Nietzsche.

THE BIRTH OF TRAGEDY/NIETZSCHE

As his title indicates, N. is trying to understand what leads to tragedy as an art form (not to tragedy necessarily in our everyday lives). I know from other English classes I've taken that lots of people have tried to figure out tragedy and written all kinds of theories about it. It's not a simple idea, really. We talked in class a lot about Aristotle's idea of tragedy—with a tragic hero, tragic flaw, reversal, catharsis. I wonder how N.'s theory compares?

The title also raises the word "birth" which is an image that comes up a lot in the text.

N. basically says tragedy comes from the birth of two ideas about art that are alike and very different at the same time. He compares this to people, who at times fight, at others agree, and yet manage to come together to procreate.

THE BIRTH OF TRAGEDY/NIETZSCHE (cont.)

The two ideas about art are related to the Greek gods Apollo and Dionysus. A. is associated with sculpture, and D. is associated with music. I can see in this case, how these are alike and different at the same time. They are both forms of art, but sculpture is something that produces an object, like a statue, while music doesn't produce anything you can actually hold and see. Music, I guess, you experience, rather than make. I wonder if those differences are what N. is seeing lead to tragedy—that you make a tragedy, like a play, but you also experience it, like music.

What really confused me about this piece, and still does, is what Apollonian and Dionysian means. N. uses those terms all the time, and I looked them up in the dictionary and didn't find anything. These terms are obviously important to this whole idea, and I'm concerned I don't know what they mean. Obviously, they relate to Dionysus and Apollo, but how, exactly?

5. Follow Up: Get Help

In writing this response, you might have noted certain ideas or aspects of the text that particularly confused you. At the same time, though, take a moment to be pleased with how much you can in fact come to understand, in spite of those sections that are still troublesome. That's a whole lot more than if you had just given up at the first line.

Having identified certain troubling or confusing parts of the text, you can now get some help. You can, for example, try to find other books and source materials that cover similar topics. Check the back of the assigned text to see if there is a bibliography or list of suggested reading. You can also go to the library or a bookstore and scan the shelves that hold books on the same subject area. Go look at other textbooks, academic encyclopedias, study guides, specialty dictionaries, and other books on the same subject.

You might get lucky and find a book or article that covers the exact same material; if you're really lucky, it will be written in much simpler language that makes the whole topic easier to understand. Even if you find sources that are equally complex, these can help you to better understand the original text. For example, other sources might describe the same material in a different way, using different illustrations and examples to describe the same overall principles. By reading more than one source on the same topic, you gain a fuller explanation and a more complete understanding of it.

You can also discuss the reading assignment with fellow students. Reading assignments are not graded, so there's no reason why you can't work together with friends. Perhaps a fellow student just happens to have a better understanding of this particular subject than you do. If this is the case, you can ask the student questions about the text to help you understand it. It's important, though, that you have a *discussion* with the student about the text rather than allow him or her to explain everything to you. Ask questions and express your own opinions and thoughts about the text. Having a conversation like this ensures that you listen carefully to the other student and also think more about the text for yourself.

Even if other students don't have a firm grasp on the material, discussing the text together may help you come to a better understanding of it. Try taking turns attempting to "teach" sections of the text to one another; very often, in the process of trying to explain something to another person, you also manage to explain it to yourself.

Finally, you can always ask your professor for extra help: however, only do this if you really need the help. Don't ask for help on every assignment. You don't want to give the impression that you are too lazy to do the work and can't think for yourself. If you decide to ask for help, go see your professor during office hours or after class and say, "I'm having trouble understanding 'Source X'. I wonder if you can recommend some other sources that I might read that could provide more information about the subject." By asking for more sources rather than an explanation of the material, you are indicating to the professor that you are willing to work to understand the text on your own. Then, in addition to recommending sources, the professor may ask you where you are having

Get help. Turn to other sources for additional information. Add to your response based on what you find out.

trouble and offer advice and detailed explanations. Whatever you do, do not complain about how hard or boring a reading assignment is — nothing makes a worse impression!

After getting help from other sources, you can either add to your initial response, or write additional notes in the left-hand margin, explaining or building upon points covered already in the first response.

Here is an additional section to the sample response, after the student did some research to get more information on confusing elements:

Okay, so I decided to try to find out more about what Apollonian and Dionysian mean. First, I looked in an Encyclopedia on Mythology. I didn't find out much there about these particular terms, but I did find out more about Apollo and Dionysus that seems relevant. According to the book, Apollo is connected with the sun, is a patron of the arts and leader of the muses, the goddesses of art and creativity. Dionysus was really interesting. He's the god of wine and fertility, and he had this devoted cult who would dance and get drunk and go crazy while worshipping him.

Next, I went to the library, and looked up "Drama, Theory" in the card catalog. When I got to the shelves, there were tons of books. I flipped through some that were really tough and confusing. But then, I found one that was so clear and helpful I couldn't believe it. It was a book on

American drama of all things! And it had this very clear summary of Nietzsche and his influence on Eugene O'Neill in one of the chapters. It said that Apollonian is related to the civilized and rational parts of Greek culture, while Dionysian relates to the more primitive and emotional aspects. It also said that N. argued Dionysus relates to the function of the chorus in Greek tragedy. The chorus is supposed to serve as the mediator between the audience and the characters in the play, helping the audience identify with the characters. This is like that cult worship of D. I read about before, when people got so frenzied, they forget who they were and felt at one with the god D.

We started talking about these ideas in class. I asked the prof. how this compares to Aristotle. He said that there's a big difference; N. doesn't emphasize fatal flaws. He shows how these characters are prey to their big egos, and that the plays show the natural patterns of life in which people inevitably fall. And since the audience is supposed to identify with the characters through the chorus, the tragedies are in a way about collective, universal experiences we all share, rather than just these big heroes.

A Note on Poorly Written Texts

If you are having trouble with a text, it won't necessarily be because it is difficult; it may just be poorly written. Don't assume that just because a professor assigned a text it has to be good. Many textbooks are mediocre in quality, sloppily thrown together, written without much insight or concern for detail.

You should learn how to become a critic of the materials you are assigned to read. This means evaluating texts for yourself by reading them with a more critical eye. Have key terms been clearly defined? Is the text organized in a clear, logical fashion? Are there detailed explanations of important terms and concepts? Did the author provide detailed illustrations and examples to support various arguments, concepts, and points? Is information factually correct?

If you deem a particular text is poor, feel free to find alternative sources. Go to the library and check the subject catalog for other material on the same topic. If your assigned text includes a bibliography or suggested reading list, try to find some of these sources. They might be better written than the original text.

When you don't like the assigned textbook for your course, you can try to find another one. Check the library or a bookstore. There will usually be several textbooks available for basic college courses. Consider buying another textbook to have on hand throughout the semester.

If you use an alternative source, make certain you compare it to the original assigned. Look at the headings and key terms in the original and check to see that the same topics are covered in the alternate source.

Word Power: Special Tips for Improving Your Vocabulary

5

*O*ne's ability to read quickly — and to comprehend what is read — in many ways relates to the extent and range of one's vocabulary. Often when we read, it's possible to skip over words we don't know because we can still understand the overall meaning of the text. However, the greater the number of unfamiliar words we encounter in a text, the less likely it will be that we can fully appreciate its meaning. And our overall reading rate will slow significantly if we have to stop and ponder these words.

When it comes to reading for school, you're especially likely to encounter many new words you won't necessarily hear in everyday conversation. For one thing, academic texts, such as books, articles, and essays, are generally written in a more sophisticated style featuring words common in academia but that you wouldn't necessarily have come across before. At the same time, each individual field of study will usually have certain words and terms associated with it that you'll come across in readings and classes within that subject. As we noted in the last chapter, you might have to stop to look up these words just to be able to understand these texts, which can slow down your reading speed. On the other hand, if you take the time to learn these words at the time you initially encounter them, then the next time you see them, you'll be able to keep on reading without delay.

Rather than merely looking up words once and then forgetting them, you can work to make these terms part of your general vocabulary; that will make it much easier to recall and understand them on future readings. In this chapter, you'll read about a strategy to improve your overall vocabulary. This will first and foremost help increase your reading speed and comprehension.

At the same time, expanding your vocabulary has other important benefits. It can help you improve your chances for exam success. Many exam questions, regardless of the subject matter, will be worded in a sophisticated, academic style that includes certain new words. Your teacher, who is writing the exam questions, is familiar with the more sophisticated terms used to discuss his or her chosen field. There's a good chance, therefore, that those words will somehow be incorporated into different exam questions. In addition, if you can incorporate more sophisticated words into your essays — whether they be term papers or examination essays — you will sound more intelligent and your teacher will likely be more impressed by your writing.

It's worth it to work on expanding your vocabulary. The more extensive your vocabulary, the faster you'll read and the more you'll understand.

And finally, like it or not, a person's vocabulary is often a sign of intelligence; people are always impressed when someone can correctly use "SAT" words in writing and conversation. Think what that can mean in a job interview or at an important work-related meeting. By improving and building your vocabulary now, you not only improve your reading speed and comprehension, but gain knowledge that can help with career success.

This chapter outlines a general strategy for improving your overall vocabulary. You should not think of this as a single task, necessary only on those occasions when you must learn a new word for an exam or to read an individual article. The aim here is for you to expand in general the number of words you know and use. Your increased vocabulary can then help you in many areas.

Improving your vocabulary involves several components. First, you have to seek out new words worth learning (unless you are specifically given words by your teacher, as is often the case with foreign language classes). Then, you need to make the effort to learn and memorize the words. Finally, you need to get in the habit of using the words so that you do not forget them. These various components are discussed in more detail in this chapter.

Discovering New Words

If you want to improve your vocabulary, you first need to identify new words to learn. You could simply sit with a dictionary and go page by page, trying to memorize every word with its definition, but you'd be lucky to finish even the letter "A" within your lifetime. As we all know, there are certain words more commonly used than others. The ones most worth knowing are the ones you probably encounter or use yourself — in conversation, in readings, in school, or at your job.

There are also certain words that are commonly used only in particular contexts and situations. In general, there are certain more sophisticated words commonly used in academia — words professors use in lecturing to their classes, in talking to one another about their professions, and in their own writing, as well as words you'll find in academic texts, like textbooks and articles. These are the words that are often on the SAT, because, while not used in most everyday conversation, they do tend to crop up in academic discussions and texts.

At the same time, when it comes to specific school subjects, you'll find there are certain words and terms that are favored by those working in those areas. When you read texts for those courses, or listen to professors teaching those classes, you might start to hear these words over and over. Very often, the professors or authors will assume that you are as familiar with the term as they are, so they won't bother to provide you with the definition. You might just let the term slide by without bothering to find out its meaning for yourself. However, chances are you'll encounter it

Keep track of new words that you come across while reading or studying particular subjects, or going to classes.

again — perhaps even on a test — and will wish you knew it. It's well worth it to you to become familiar with the "lingo" of whatever subject you are studying.

To narrow down your search for new words, then, you should begin compiling lists of these words as they come up in various contexts. To do that, you might consider keeping a special log book of new words. You can divide the book into sections — one big section for new words you encounter in general (such as in the newspaper, in conversation, or in pleasure reading), and separate sections for each course you are taking. As you come across new words, you can list them in the proper section.

In addition to finding words in your everyday reading and in your coursework, you might consider some other sources for new words. There are several calendars on the market that provide you with one new word a day. You could purchase one and add those words to your log book. You also might try doing crossword puzzles, which are filled with interesting, sophisticated words.

To get you started, here's a list of vocabulary words that are often used in written academic works. You'll probably encounter these words in some of your reading assignments for school. For each word, there's a concise definition and an example of the word used in a sentence, which, as is discussed in the next section, is an important part of the process of learning new words.

evince— to display clearly, show or reveal
A detailed study of these two plays will *evince* many similarities between them.

formulate— to put into a set statement or expression, to devise (as in a policy or plan)
The novel's theme is *formulated* in the final chapter.

fortuitous— lucky, happening by chance, accidental
It was certainly *fortuitous* that they ran into each other in London.

germane— relevant, appropriate to, fitting
A discussion of bone structure is certainly *germane* to our study of anatomy.

hegemony— those persons or institutions in power over others
The church was a *hegemonic* institution in the Middle Ages.

heinous— shockingly evil and hateful
Richard III is the most *heinous* of Shakespeare's villains.

illuminate— to make clear, shed light on
This paper will *illuminate* the specific connections between the author's life and work.

ingenuous— showing innocent and child-like simplicity and candor; noble and honest, trusting
She is so *ingenuous*, she will trust just about anyone.

juxtapose— to place side by side for the sake of comparison
If we *juxtapose* a painting by Van Gogh with one by Matisse, their similar use of color becomes clear.

manifest— to make evident or certain by showing or displaying

His concern for the underprivileged has been made *manifest* many times by his extensive volunteer work.

ontological— relating to the nature of existence and our knowledge of it

Her writings have taken an *ontological* twist now that she has begun to discuss more personal issues.

perspicacity— acute mental power; shrewdness

Your adept performance in that oral examination demonstrated your *perspicacity*.

plethora— an abundance or excess

To prove my point, I will raise a *plethora* of sources and pieces of evidence.

praxis— customary action or practice

It is usually easier to understand something in *praxis* rather than theory.

preponderance— a majority; a superiority in power, importance, number, or strength

In the election, she has a *preponderance* of devoted followers.

prevalent— widespread; generally accepted, seen or favored

Signs that the economy is not doing well are certainly *prevalent*.

Learning New Words

In addition to compiling your lists of words, you need to make the effort to learn what they mean and memorize them; after all, lists of words that are meaningless won't really help you much. You can, if you like, look up words as soon as you initially see them and immediately copy them with their definitions into your log book. By doing this, you have the benefit of immediately seeing the word used in some context; knowing a word's meaning also might help make the rest of your reading more understandable.

However, looking up and memorizing every single new word you encounter while you are trying to read is not always necessary, nor is it always helpful. Some words might be rather obscure and not worth the time and effort to memorize. If you wait until you complete an entire reading assignment, or several assignments, you can then see which words are repeated. Those are the ones well worth studying. (If you find you just cannot understand the reading without knowing what a particular word means, it is then worth it to look it up at *that* moment.) Looking up new words as you come across them can slow down the reading process and detract from your ability to follow the flow of the argument. However, jotting down the word on a list only takes a second. So make it a practice to at least note the new words you encounter while reading. You can then return to your lists of words later and begin looking up their definitions. You could look up all the words when you've completed a particular reading assignment, or

Make it a special point to look up definitions for new words that seem particularly important or are repeated. You can do this when you first encounter the word, or set aside time each week to go over a list of new words.

you might set aside some time each week. Try to set a goal for yourself of learning a set number of new words each week, perhaps five to ten, and set aside a specific time to do so. You could then flip through your book and select the five to ten, words that seem to have been the most important during your reading for that week and concentrate most on learning those words.

Each time you look up a new word, you should jot down a brief definition of it in your log book. Remember to use a good, college-level dictionary, one that will include more words you're likely to find in academic subject areas. You do not need to copy down the entire definition. Dictionary definitions can be quite wordy. You can usually jot down just two or three words that will convey the essential meaning of the word. For example, if you look up the word *superfluous*, the definition reads, "exceeding what is sufficient or necessary; marked by wastefulness." You could simply jot down "excess; wasteful" and get the general sense of the word.

Additionally, the dictionary may list several definitions for a word, from the more prevalent to the more obscure. In most cases, only the more prevalent ones will be important; those are the ones you'll want to write down.

Write a brief definition of each word you look up, if possible using only one to three words. Write several sentences using the word correctly in context.

After writing down the definition of the word, you need to make the effort to memorize it, so you'll be able to use it later on. When you initially encounter a new piece of information, it is stored in your short-term memory. The short-term memory can only hold items of information for a brief period of time (such as a phone number you've just looked up in the phone book). To remember something at a much later point in time, the information must be transferred to your long-term memory. To do so, you must make an active effort to learn the information with the goal of remembering it later on. As with the reading strategies discussed here, you cannot memorize passively. Just staring at long lists of words and assuming you'll remember them won't work. You need to make memorization an active process.

Here are some *mnemonic devices* specifically designed to help you remember words and their definitions. A mnemonic device is any strategy you use to help improve your memorization of a specific piece of information. For each of the suggested mnemonics below, you'll see that you need to do something active, which is what makes them effective. (For a more extensive discussion of improving memory, see *Test-Taking Secrets* in the Backpack Study Series.)

Cue Cards

Cue cards are an excellent way to memorize and test yourself on new words. Simply put the word on one side of an index card, and write its brief definition on the other. You then should spend time quizzing yourself on the stack of cards. Run through the stack of cards, looking at each word and then saying its definition out loud. For each one you get wrong, make a special effort to remember it (perhaps by repeating the word and its definition several times out loud, or writing it down several times, or creating a rhyme or other link as discussed in the next sections). You also should test yourself in reverse, looking at the definitions and trying to recall the words. Each time you successfully test yourself on a batch of five to ten words, you can add the cards to the bigger stack of all the new words you've been learning. Every once in a while, test yourself on the entire stack to see how many you can remember.

Rhymes or Alliteration

It is much easier to remember a word's definition if you can find definitions that rhyme with the word or share the same first few letters. For example, the definition of the word *paradigm* is "an outstandingly clear or typical example or pattern." You can simply remember though that a "paradigm" is a "pattern," which starts with the same two letters. Similarly, you can remember the word *veracity* as meaning "honesty," as the "ty" ending makes them sound similar.

> Use mnemonic devices like alliteration and visualization to help you remember definitions.

Associative Links

One of the reasons it is difficult to remember information is that, even if we have learned it and stored it in long-term memory, we can't access it. Our long-term memories are like walk-in closets; they can hold an awful lot of stuff, but it's sometimes hard to find exactly what you're looking for in all the clutter.

To help access information in long-term memory, scientists and psychologists have found that it helps to have some kind of associative link. This is a word or image connected to the piece of information you are hoping to remember. By thinking of that word or image, you immediately "pull up" the additional information you're looking for. Visual associations are particularly strong, as it's easier to recall a picture than word.

To create visual associative links, you should examine words or parts of words and create visual images that you associate with the definition of the word. For example, if you want to remember that the word *imperious* means arrogant or domineering, you could examine the word and focus on the word "imp" at the start of it. You could them picture a rather snobby "imp." In the future, when you see the word *imperious*, you'll get a mental flash of that snobby imp, and thereby remember the definition.

VOCABULARY MEMORIZATION PRACTICE EXERCISE

Go back to the sample list of vocabulary words and definitions earlier in this chapter and try to come up with a mnemonic device to help you remember each word. Wait a few hours and then try to write their definitions down here, using whatever mnemonic devices you made for yourself. How many were you able to remember? If you need help coming up with mnemonic devices, you can look at the suggestions for verbal and visual associative links on the following pages.

formulate —	praxis —
germane —	prevalent —
heinous —	fortuitous —
preponderance —	juxtapose —
evince —	perspicacity —
illuminate —	manifest —
hegemony —	ingenuous —
ontological —	plethora —

Here's another example: *Perspicacious* means smart, keen, shrewd. The first several letters of the word — "perspi" — are the same as in the word *perspire*. To learn what the word means, you can visualize someone on a TV quiz show perspiring beneath the hot lights — an image of a smart *perspicacious* person that is linked with the word *perspire*.

By the way, this method can be particularly helpful when you attempt to memorize definitions of words in a foreign language. Even though the original word is not in English, you can usually identify English words (or parts of words) within the foreign word and use them to create visual images. For example, in French, the word *lapin* means rabbit. You can see the English word *lap* in the French word, and then visualize a warm, cuddly rabbit nested in your lap.

Sample Mnemonic Devices

(NOTE: the key word(s) from the definition that each verbal/visual link connects with is listed in italics).

evince— shares the same initial letters as the word "evil," and in mysteries, the evil villain is always *revealed* in the end.

formulate— is similar to the word "formula" and to create a new formula, you must *have some kind of plan*. Also, you can picture an application "form" for buying a new house that includes a floor *plan* of the new place.

fortuitous— shares the same first letters as the word "fortune." You can visualize a lottery ticket (maybe even for the number forty to emphasize the "fort" link) that will provide the *lucky* winner with a "fortune," totally *by chance*.

germane— can be broken down into the words "germ" and "man," and germs are *relevant to* man's health. You can also picture a famous "German" man (such as Hegel or Thomas Mann) whose work was *relevant* to his country.

hegemony— starts with the letters and sound of the word "hedge"; you can picture a very tall "hedge" that reaches high *above* other people, holding them in its sway. The end of the word is "money," which also holds tremendous power over people.

heinous— begins with "hein" which is similar to "heinz"; you can picture a bottle of Heinz ketchup that has gone bad and become a dark horrible color, looking particularly *nasty*, even *hateful*. You also might link the word with "hell," which shares the same first two letters, and is also a *shockingly evil and hateful* place.

illuminate— starts with the word "ill," and when someone is ill, a doctor tries to *shed light* on what's wrong with them; also, the sick person might have a fever and be pale, as if *lit by a bright light*.

ingenuous— starts with the letters "ingen" which sounds like the slang word "injun" and an *innocent children*'s game is "cowboys and injuns." Also, part of the word is similar to "generous," and to be generous to a panhandler is a *noble* thing indicating you trust the person's sob story.

juxtapose— includes the word "pose." You can picture a "posed" model who has had her hair styled next to a picture of her before the makeover — an image of *a side-by-side comparison*.

manifest— ends with the letters "fest" which are the start of the word "festival." At a wedding festival, the couple's love for one another is *displayed and made evident*; it is also similar to the word "feast" when the mounds of food are also put on *display*. Also, the first few letters are "mani" as in the word "maniac"; to put a "maniac" in jail, you need to provide *evidence* of his terrible behavior.

ontological— includes the words "onto" and "logical"; wondering about our *existence*— how we got "onto" the earth — is a "logical" question to ask.

perspicacity— starts with the same letters as "perspiring," and you can picture a *smart* person perspiring while on a TV quiz show.

plethora— shares the same first few letters as "plenty"; having "plenty" of something means it's in *abundance*.

praxis— includes the word "axis"; figure skaters who can do a triple "axis" must *practice* a great deal.

preponderance— includes the word "pond"; you can picture a pond that is overflowing with fish, which means it has a *greater number* and more *importance* than other, empty ponds.

prevalent— includes the word "vale" which sounds the same as "veil"; you can picture a bride's flowing veil, which is *widespread* about her and *generally seen* by everyone at the wedding.

Word Breakdown

As you study words, it can often be tremendously helpful to break them down into smaller parts. You can do this by identifying prefixes and suffixes. A prefix refers to a word element that is added to the start of a word that changes or enhances its meaning. Suffixes are added to the ends of words, and similarly add or change meanings. For example, *mistrust* includes the prefix "mis" added to the word "trust." By placing the prefix "mis" in front of trust, you change the word, making it mean NOT to trust someone. Similarly, adding "ology" to certain words (or parts of words) indicates the "study of" some subject. For example, *sociology* is derived from a form of the word "society" and "ology."

There are certain common prefixes and suffixes with which you can become familiar. That way, whenever you see them, you can have some sense of what the word means, even if you don't know the word itself. That might help, for example, on exams; if you encounter words with which you are unfamiliar but do know the meaning of a prefix or suffix of the word, you may be able to gain a sense of the word's connotation. At the very least, it might help you figure out the gist of whatever question contains the word. Additionally, when you try to memorize words with familiar prefixes or suffixes, you don't have to work as hard, as you already know the meaning of part of them.

Following is a list of some common prefixes and suffixes. You can also start noting others and identify them in your log book.

PREFIXES

pre-	earlier than, prior to, before (as in preview and prewar)
post-	afterward, later (as in postgame show)
arch-	chief, principal (as in archenemy)
co-	joint, with, together (as in cocreator or cowriter)
neo-	new, newly formed, recent (as in neoimpressionism)
pseudo-	false, phony (as in pseudonym)
de-	do the opposite, reverse, remove, reduce (as in deemphasize)
mis-	wrongly, badly (as in misuse and misbehave)
dis-	do the opposite of, undo (as in disassociate and disavow)
sub-	under, beneath, below (as in subordinate and subpar)
proto-	first, beginning, giving rise to others (as in prototype)
non-	not, other than, reverse of (as in nonsense and nonabrasive)

SUFFIXES

-nomy	system of laws governing or sum of knowledge about (as in astronomy)
-ism	an act, practice, or process (as in criticism and plagiarism)
-ate	acted upon, marked by having, affected by (as in fortunate)
-ous	full of, filled with, abounding in (as in poisonous and treasonous)

> Get in the habit of using new words you learn, especially ones that are important to particular subjects. The more you use it, the better you'll remember it. If you fail to use it, you will lose it.

Use It or Lose It

Once you have successfully identified and memorized the definitions of new words, it is crucial that you begin to use them — and use them frequently. The more you use words, the more easily accessed they become. That means in future readings you'll treat these new words the same way you would such familiar words as mom or the. You'll see them, already know what they mean, and just keep on reading. However, long periods of disuse means the words get lost somewhere in your long-term memory and are harder to recall.

When you first write down a word's definition, you might want to immediately brainstorm and write down a few sentences that use the word. This will get you in the habit of actually using the word and help you become familiar with the contexts in which the word might come up. Next, try to use the word in conversation or in your writing. This, of course, will be easier to do with some words than with others. However, you will probably have occasion to use many words you discover in your school assignments. You can use them when asking questions of your professor, in your homework assignments, and on essays and exams.

Managing Your Reading Load

Overcoming the Time Crunch

As we noted earlier in the book, you are sometimes going to have many more reading assignments than you can possibly handle in a given week. Your teachers are, after all, giving you reading assignments without any sense of the workload you have in other classes. Inevitably, you'll have weeks where there are long, difficult readings due in all of your classes, or when you have tons of other commitments and responsibilities that tie up your time. Unless you've got a bionic eye, you're just physically not going to be able to do all the required reading for that week — much less understand it, take notes, and write responses.

Don't despair. There are ways in which you can make your reading load manageable!

There are two major strategies for grappling with that heavy reading load. One is to learn how to read faster using speed-reading techniques. Those techniques are discussed in detail in the next chapter. Be aware, though, that learning to read faster takes time and practice. Speed-reading therefore won't necessarily be a feasible option for you, especially early on in your academic career, before you've had a chance to learn, practice, and hone these skills.

You can start being a *selective* reader, however. Being a selective reader means making intelligent and informed decisions for yourself about what you can and should read. It means that although you may not read everything, you will think carefully about what you do read, learn from it, retain it, and be able to use it.

Making Educated Decisions:
Selective Reading Guidelines

The most basic principle of being a selective reader is that you make educated decisions about what to read carefully, what to skim, and what not to read at all. But you need to be smart about your decisions. You don't want to ignore a source that is crucial to your understanding of the topic. You also don't want to cut a source you are likely to be tested on.

You need to at least glance through each source to get a sense of its contents so that you can make an educated decision. Based on your sense of what is covered in the text, your time frame, and your previous knowledge of the topic, you can make decisions about what to read.

Here are some decisions you might make:

- Read some assignments and save others for when you have more time, or cut them out all together.

> If you're pressed for time and cannot do all of your required reading assignments, you can still read selectively. Reading selectively means making smart choices about what to read carefully, what to skim, and what to cut.

- Read the entire text very carefully, just skim it, or ignore it completely.
- Read some sections of the text very carefully, and skim others.
- Only read sections of the text that are new to you; if sections rehash terms and concepts you already know about, skip them.
- Only read sections of the text that you know are relevant to the material covered in the course. For example, if you see sections that reflect things your professor has discussed in class or reflect topics listed on the syllabus, you probably should read those.
- Rather than read all assigned texts for all of your classes, only read the most important texts for each course.

Making the Cuts: How to Prioritize Your Reading List

Some of the reading assignments you receive are going to be extremely important. The entire classroom lecture or discussion might center on certain readings; if you don't do them, you'll be completely lost in class and your teacher might lower your grade for failure to participate. Worse, there may be a reading assignment that leads to specific questions on an exam. On the other hand, there may be many more assignments that are not nearly as relevant or important. They might merely rehash material already discussed in class, or supplement important topics.

As you gain a sense of what sources are the most important, you can make intelligent decisions about what to read. You can then prioritize your readings. Prioritizing means doing the most important reading assignments first, and doing the others later when you have more time.

In general, you should probably read primary sources over secondary sources. A primary source is a work written directly by the author, such as works of literature like plays and novels, historical documents, treatises, theories, and lab reports. A secondary source is anything written about a primary source, such as textbooks, journal articles, term papers, and reviews. A primary source would be an article written by Freud; a secondary source would be an article *about* the article by Freud. Primary sources are usually more central to classroom discussion and lectures and therefore are more worth reading. You're more likely to be lost in a class if you haven't read a primary source that is the topic of discussion. Questions about primary sources are also likely to show up on an exam.

While reading all primary sources should be a priority, it might not always be feasible. To help you out when you're in a bind, you might be able to track down a summary of a

Prioritize your overall reading list. Glance through different assignments and try and get a sense of how relevant or significant they are to the course. First read the more important works.

particular primary source. For example, there are several student guides to works of literature that you can buy in most bookstores. In the reference section of the library, you will also find various encyclopedias and dictionaries that summarize major works by various writers, scientists, historians, and theoreticians (ask the librarian where to find them). You should, however,\ only refer to these summaries and student guides if you are *really* pressed for time. Reading a summary never takes the place of reading the actual source. In fact, some summaries overlook important information and can give you a misleading impression about what is covered. If you use a summary, you should try to read the primary source sometime before the exam so you can be prepared to answer questions about it in detail.

In addition to evaluating which texts are most important to read for *each* course, you may also want to compare assignments *between* courses. Each week, look at the reading assignments for all your courses. You may decide to read the most important texts in each course and skim or ignore others. Or, you might find it is valuable to do all the reading for one particular course, while it is not necessary for others. Some professors rely heavily on outside reading assignments and assume students keep up with the reading, while others consider reading secondary to the lectures. As the semester goes on, you will get a sense for how important your professor thinks the reading assignments are.

You can also prioritize your reading within assignments; certain sections of a chapter or an essay might be more important and relevant than others. You can read first those sections you deem most important or relevant. If you then find you have more time available, you can read others. If you see anything that your professor has previously mentioned, or anything that you know will be covered in class, that might be your priority as far as what to read. Similarly, you might want to prioritize things you don't know over things with which you are already familiar.

As you make decisions about what to cut, remember that you can always go back and read a text (or part of a text) that you decided to skip. If, for example, you find that your professor discusses a text in detail during a lecture, you should make certain you go back and read it more carefully. If you discover you have free time or a week when the reading assignments are relatively light, you may want to use the time to catch up on previous assignments.

Skimming Texts

Rather than not read a text at all, you may decide to skim it; you can skim the entire text, or just parts of it. Skimming a text is really a form of selective reading. To skim, read the entire selection from start to finish at a slightly faster pace than you would normally read. You can freely skip certain words,

> You can always go back and reread a text more carefully at some point when you feel less pressure and have the time. Just be certain you do this before a major exam on which you might be quizzed about the text.

phrases, or sentences. You do, though, want to spot and stop to read anything that seems particularly important. These sections, you can read more slowly, and give them more thought.

The best way to skim a text is to stop to read the following sections more carefully.

Introductions, Conclusions, Summary Paragraphs

You should read the introduction and conclusion of each text in its entirety, as these paragraphs usually outline the most important points covered in the text. You might also look for "summary paragraphs." These are paragraphs within the text that summarize smaller sections of the text rather than the whole thing. If a text is divided into topics and subtopics, each with its own heading, these sections might have their own introductions and conclusions. As you skim, be on the lookout for terms such as "in conclusion," "to sum up," and "therefore" that indicate the author is summarizing various points.

First and Last Lines of Paragraphs

If you go through a text and read just the first and last line of each paragraph, you will get an adequate concept

Skim all or part of a text; this can help you save time, and it is better than not reading at all. To skim, read the passage at a faster pace, skipping certain words and phrases. Take the time, though, to read first and last lines of paragraphs, summaries, and key terms, and look at pictures and diagrams.

of what the text covers. The first line of many paragraphs will introduce the topic covered, while the last line will often summarize the contents of the paragraph or serve as a transition to the next paragraph. As you read first and last sentences, you might come across a line that indicates a paragraph is particularly important or intriguing. If that happens, go ahead and read some of the entire paragraph.

Pictures, Charts, and Diagrams

Just as first and last sentences of paragraphs often sum up key points, pictures, charts, and diagrams usually correspond to key information conveyed in the text. Look over all of these and read the captions for them.

Sample of a Skimmed Textbook Entry

The following is a page from a chapter of a textbook. The highlighted sections indicate the parts you would read if you were skimming the chapter. As an exercise, try reading just the highlighted section. Do you still manage to get a general sense of the content of this chapter?

EARLY BRITISH HISTORY AND CULTURE
•••••••••••••••••••••••••••••••••••••••

In this chapter, we will trace the early history of Britain, from the Anglo-Saxon conquest, circa 450, through the Norman Conquest in 1066. We will also explore the effects of these two invasions on British life, culture, and literature.

THE ANGLO-SAXON INVASION AND THE HEROIC IDEAL

In the first half of the fifth century, around the year 450, groups of people known as the **ANGLO-SAXONS** invaded the isle of Britain. At that time, Britain was inhabited by a group known as the **CELTS.** This so-called invasion was the latest in a series of migrations that had started years before. These migrations involved a series of Germanic tribes from the northeast of Europe who moved into areas of the Roman Empire in the west, south, and southeast. The Anglo-Saxon invaders actually consisted of three tribes—**THE ANGLES, THE SAXONS, AND THE JUTES.** Although they were independent, these three tribes shared a common Germanic heritage that helped unite them.

According to Germanic heritage, society was originally organized by the family unit. The head of the family was the **CHIEF** of all his close kinsmen. As time passed, that social unit grew; numbers of families became united under a **KING,** derived from the Germanic word for chief. However, the kingships still were relatively small and quite unstable. Thus, even after the Anglo-Saxons settled in Britain, the island was still broken up into many different, constantly shifting kingdoms.

Central to the kingship system was a notion of ideal kingly behavior that is generally referred to as the **HEROIC IDEAL.** Kings were supposed to prove themselves worthy of their leadership roles, particularly by showing their skill and courage in battle. These qualities when found in a king provided a sense of stability at a time when life was anything but stable. The heroic ideal also came to refer to the warriors who served the king and attempted to mirror his behavior and earn his favor. The Anglo-Saxons brought the heroic ideal with them to Britain and it became a part of English culture and tradition. As we will see, this heroic ideal is a central aspect of Old English literary works such as Beowulf.

THE NORMAN CONQUEST

As we have seen, in the early half of the middle ages, the inhabitants of Britain lacked any kind of stable societal organization. That all changed in 1066, the year of the **NORMAN CONQUEST.**

In 1066, Britain was once again invaded by a Germanic tribe, but one very different from the Anglo-Saxons. These people were known as the **NORMANS,** and they were descendants of Scandinavian adventurers who had seized a wide part of northern France at the start of the tenth century. Although the Norman rulers' leader, **WILLIAM,** was a subject of the king of France, Normandy was very much an independent entity. The invasion of England was led by William. Still largely divided, the English were easily overthrown at the **BATTLE OF HASTINGS.** William's forces went on to take over England and he became its king.

Words and Phrases in Boldface or Italics

These terms are generally key terms or major concepts involving important new information. If you do not know the term and it seems significant, read the entire sentence, or the entire section. Those words and phrases are often the most important pieces of information in a text.

Follow Up

You should still take the time to take notes and/or write a response on what you read selectively, even if you are skimming, using techniques described in earlier chapters of this book. As you read or skim selected sections, you will still be exposed to new material and ideas you will want to retain. Taking notes and writing a response will help you do that. If you are pressed for time, you can write a very quick response. Set a time limit for yourself of five or ten minutes and write as much as you can about what you just read, particularly noting any general themes and topics covered. If there were many key terms in the assignment you know you need to understand and remember, either make a list of them while you read, or go back and reread the section at some point when you have more time and can take notes. Just remember to do this before any exam.

Reading for Speed

Reading selectively can help you out on specific assignments when you face a time crunch. In general, though, there are several ways to improve your overall reading rate. This chapter describes some strategies and techniques for improving your reading speed. However, it is extremely important that you understand *it takes time and work to increase your reading speed.* Don't expect to read this chapter and immediately flip through a required textbook reading in a few minutes.

Another problem is that, while the techniques described here do improve reading speed, they don't guarantee full comprehension or retention of the material. Speed-reading will give you an overall sense of the material — an idea, for example, of the main topics that are covered. Having that understanding is certainly better than not having read at all; you can still attend class and follow a lecture or discussion about the material. You may even be able to get through some exam questions based on that reading experience. But you generally won't get the same details nor will you absorb, understand, and retain as much material as when you use the active reading techniques discussed earlier in the book.

With time and practice, you can both increase your speed and your ability to understand and retain something you've read. When you become comfortable with the strategies described here, you can apply them to certain required reading assignments, especially during weeks when you are overloaded and cannot use the strategies discussed earlier on every assignment. As with selective reading, though, you can always go back and reread a text — and take notes on it — more carefully. You should make it a point to do this for any text you sense is especially important for your course and on which you will likely be questioned at exam time.

It's a good idea for you to practice these techniques when you have long stretches of time off from school — summer vacations, weekends, winter breaks. You should also practice with reading materials that are not required for classes. That way you can work on increasing your speed without necessarily worrying about having to understand and retain what you read for a particular class. At the end of this section, you'll find a program for working on speed-reading during free time with books you choose.

Stop Sounding Words Out

Remember when you were a kid and you learned how to "recite" your ABCs? After learning the alphabet, you probably learned how to read whole words and then sentences by "sounding them out" out loud. Eventually, you moved on to longer passages, but were still encouraged to sound out words out loud as you read.

Most people, in fact, learn how to read by reading out loud — and that can cause problems later on when it comes to trying to read quickly. After reading out loud for a period, we are encouraged to begin to "read to ourselves" silently. While many people eventually learn to read without sounding out the words, many others have difficulty making the transition. Some people still feel the need to read out loud, especially on a difficult sentence or passage. Others merely whisper to themselves or move their lips as they read. And others, while not moving their mouths, are still reading "out loud" in their minds, hearing themselves say each word, rather than just visually taking in the information they see on the page through the eyes.

Reading in this manner severely slows down one's reading rate. That's because spoken speech, which involves physical movement of the tongue and lips, takes more time than silently reading, which only uses the eyes and the brain. If you do read out loud or move your lips, don't feel badly about it. It's not a sign of lack of intelligence, only of a habit. You learned how to read one way and never were encouraged to move your reading to another stage. You can work to move to that level now, and you'll find your reading rate increasing significantly. It is possible you may not even be aware of it if

> Don't move your mouth or lips. Don't "sound out" words in your head. Learn to read only with your eyes, taking in words visually.

you do read out loud or move your lips. So whether or not you know you read this way, you might want to try the following exercise.

Try reading with a lollipop in your mouth (you can also bite on a pencil or on your lower lip). This will make it difficult for you to move your tongue or lips — and more importantly, it will make you aware of when you are in fact doing this. When you become aware of reading out loud or sounding out words, you then need to make a conscious effort to stop it. Force your lips to remain closed, and bite down a bit harder on the lollipop.

This technique will help you stop moving your mouth, but it won't necessarily stop you from reading the words "out loud" in your head. The trick is to read without thinking about reading. That may sound silly or even impossible, but consider how many tasks you do automatically without thinking about doing them. You might swim or hit a baseball, for example, without necessarily thinking about each action involved. And consider how much more easily you can swim or play ball by NOT thinking to yourself about what you are doing moment by moment.

Try forcing yourself to read at a faster pace than normal. Don't worry, at least when first training yourself to read faster, about understanding everything you read. By reading at a slightly faster pace, you won't have as much time to sound out words in your head. Start reading more often at this faster pace. In time, you'll find yourself just reading, without sounding out what you read. The more accustomed you become to reading silently and visually, the more it will become a comfortable old habit you just do without thinking about it.

Move It and Lose It

As we just noted, spoken speech is a physical activity that takes more time than the mental activity of reading, which involves the eyes and the brain. In addition to moving their mouths and lips, many people unnecessarily move a great deal while reading which also slows them down. Some people fidget in their chairs. Others keep lifting their heads and looking around. Others use their fingers or a ruler as a pointer, moving it across each and every line that they read. All of these movements slow down reading rate.

Whether you are lying on your bed or sitting at a desk, concentrate on moving as little as possible. Ideally, you should only need to move your eyes (and even these do not need to move that often, as we'll soon see); you can also move your fingers, but only when you turn pages, not as a pointer. Of course, if you are reading and taking notes, as we recommended above, you'll be moving a bit more. It is up to you whether or not you choose to take notes as you read. If you are in a real hurry, you may decide to reread

Minimize movements of all kinds. More only your eyes and fingertips.

something later when you can have the time to take notes. Even if you take notes, concentrate on not moving your head and body in addition to the movements necessary to read and write notes.

No Stopping and No Turning Back

If you're taking a car trip, and you have all the time in the world to get to your destination, you can go leisurely; you can feel free to stop often to take in the scenery, pulling onto side routes, randomly exploring the terrain, and even retracing your steps to return to that ice cream place you passed a few miles back. But if you're in a hurry, you're going to take a direct route, going from your house straight to your destination without stopping. The same principles hold true for speed-reading.

If you have plenty of time, you can go back and reread anything you please. If you find you've forgotten something, or you're getting confused, you can back up and reread passages. If you come across vocabulary words you do not know, you can take the time to look them up. And you can feel free to take little breaks, looking up and around the room, before getting back to the page. All of that, though, slows you down.

124

To be a speed-reader, you need to read from start to finish without stopping and definitely without going back to reread. Here are some tips for training yourself to read straight through this way:

Get a Sense of the Big Picture

As with the reading strategy we discussed earlier, it is still worth it for you to take a few minutes to scan through the material to get a sense of the big picture. To return for a moment to the car trip analogy, if you have a map and have planned your journey ahead, you can more confidently take your trip, without stopping to ponder where you are headed and how you'll get there. Similarly, by getting a general sense of what you are reading in advance, you have a big picture in mind as you read that can keep you on track. Take the time to flip through the reading assignment, getting a sense of how long it is and what topics are addressed. Look at any pictures or diagrams. Read the headings and sub-headings of different sections. Then, as you read, you'll always have a sense of where within the overall reading you are, and how much further you've got to go.

Don't Sweat the Small Stuff

As you read, you may find yourself becoming confused, losing your train of thought, or encountering material you don't understand. You still should not stop — just keep on reading. If you are trying to read as quickly as possible, you don't have the time to stop, reread sections, look up words, or ponder each paragraph. But don't worry about it. By the time you get to the end of the assignment, simply by speed-reading the entire text, you will have read and understood enough of the material to have a general sense of what was discussed. In other words, you may not have concentrated on and learned every detail of the passage — the small stuff — but you will be able to discuss the general themes and topics, which are usually more important. Keep in mind that you can always go back and reread the entire passage more carefully when you have the time.

Minimize and Ignore Distractions

Anything that distracts from your reading is going to force you to look up from the page. And if you look up, even for a split second, it is going to take time to find your place, regain your pacing, and recapture your train of thought. As with any reading you do, choose a place where you won't be bothered, and do what you can to minimize distractions. Turn off the ringer on the phone, close the window shades, shut the door — whatever will help you remain focused on the reading. Of course, inevitably there will still be distractions, no matter how hard you try to prevent them. If you are speed-reading, just do your best to ignore them and keep your eyes on the page.

Turn Pages Rapidly

It sounds silly, but turning the page can take up precious time. This is especially true if you wait until you get to the bottom of a page and then start struggling to separate it from the next page, creating an unnecessary pause and dis-

Keep reading, from the start of the text to the end, without stopping, and without rereading anything. Starting out your reading by taking a few moments to review the text and gain a sense of the big picture can help you move through it more quickly. Learn to turn pages rapidly.

rupting the flow of your reading. Get in the habit of grasping the top right-hand corner of the right page of a book while you are reading the page. When you get to the end of the page, you can then immediately turn the page and continue reading without stopping. As you become used to this routine, your fingers will do the work of separating the pages and preparing to turn the page without your having to think about it at all.

REMEMBER: Speed-reading means reading an assigned text from beginning to end *without stopping at all for any reason*.

Pace Yourself

A technique that runners use to increase their speed, and to make certain they get to the end of the race, is to maintain a steady but rapid pace. You can do the same thing as a speed-reader. As you read, you should fall into a steady, rapid rhythm. By reading with rhythm you ensure you continue to read from start to finish without stopping; you won't be so concerned if you find yourself momentarily confused by new material, and you'll maintain a steadier, uninterrupted train of thought.

You can also set a rhythm for yourself faster than your normal reading speed to help you to learn to read more quickly. As you start learning to speed-read, consciously force yourself to read a bit faster than usual. When that pace becomes comfortable, you can again force yourself to read at an even faster pace. Over time, as you become more comfortable with speed-reading skills, you can continue to set faster paces for yourself. However, when you find you are reading too fast to understand most of the material, it's time to slow down a bit and settle on that pace.

To learn how to pace yourself, you can consider buying or borrowing a metronome. That's the device that piano players use to set the beat while playing a musical composition. You can set the metronome at a particular beat; keep it on while you read and it will encourage you to read at a similar pace. When you get used to that pace, you can set it for a faster one. You can also use a timer or loud clock to set a faster pace; just hearing the ticking in the background as you read will help you keep a steady pace.

If you don't want to use a metronome, you can select music to listen to that follows a particular beat. Pick fast-paced music you are already familiar with that won't distract you from reading; just having a fast beat in the background will help you read at a faster pace.

As you become accustomed to speed-reading, you won't need props to help keep a beat. You'll be able to develop your own comfortable, fast pace and follow it.

Set a steady but rapid pace. This will help you keep reading at a fast rate without stopping.

Read Word Clumps, Not Individual Words

Many people — even when reading silently to themselves — read one word at a time, taking a short pause between words. This manner of reading is slow and unnecessary. You can learn to "take in" and understand larger clumps of words, and thus read faster.

When you look at a photograph or even watch television, you don't concentrate on each individual figure you see; instead, you take in the whole picture. Your eye may concentrate on one area, such as the center of the picture or on a particular figure, but you still "see" and have an awareness of the entire picture.

The same idea is possible with reading. You can concentrate on a section of a line of text but still take in the rest of it, even if you are not looking directly at it. By taking in larger clusters of words rather than reading one word at a time, you move your eyes less, take fewer breaks, and — you guessed it — increase your reading speed.

Try this exercise. For the following list of words, look only at the center word in bold. Start from the top line and go down to the bottom of the page, looking at the center words. Don't let your eyes move from side to side — move your eyes from the top of the page to the bottom, concentrating only on the bold words in the center of each line. Since these words are in bold, your eyes will be particularly drawn to them. Even though you are looking at the center word, see how many of the other words on the page in each line you also "take in."

uncle	**calendar**	title
school	**ocean**	subway
alligator	**sunshine**	movies
umbrella	**mittens**	stomach
penguin	**history**	bridge
light bulb	**words**	birthday
airplane	**prism**	tennis
soup	**sidewalk**	mathematics
textbook	**friend**	degree
jogging	**envelope**	nighttime
adventure	**skiing**	dinner
fourteen	**shiny**	candles
symbol	**clouds**	skate
literature	**pencil**	hearing
hungry	**shoes**	music
holiday	**peanut**	sister
bedroom	**elevator**	doorway
green	**wallet**	shampoo
computer	**brave**	occupation
graduation	**feather**	princess

Now try doing it without any bold words. Just start at the center of the first line, read downward from top to bottom, concentrating on the center section of each line, and see how much you are able to "take in."

happiness	database	brakes
postage	capital	December
quantity	telephone	wristwatch
Boston	freedom	stapler
panther	pizza	motive
earthquake	socks	newspaper
maple	combination	squash
medicine	shoehorn	antenna
inflation	hammer	clothing
Spanish	detective	spectacle
knot	armchair	banister
postcard	temperature	modem
sticker	catalog	lawyer
bookstore	goggles	island
laundry	telephone	alarm
Monday	elevator	service
village	badge	guarantee
waterfall	note	evening
photograph	concert	plumber
ticket	locomotive	bubble
siren	octopus	professor

It's even easier to read this way when you are reading complete sentences. That's because sentences are aimed at communicating a complete idea. Unlike the exercises above, they are not made up of random lists of words; the words are put in a particular order and are connected in terms of the meaning they are conveying. So even if you don't actually "read" each word in a sentence, you can still get the gist of it and essentially know what idea the sentence is expressing.

Try reading this column, again only concentrating on the words in the center of each line. Let your eyes move from the top of the section, line by line, to the bottom. Try not to move your eyes from side to side, but from top to bottom. Are you able to "take in" and understand the whole sentence?

Once	you	train
your	eye	to
read	this	new
way,	you	find
that	it	is
not	so	difficult
to	do.	

You can practice reading this way by reading the newspaper. Newspapers have very narrow columns of text, which make it easy for you to take in a whole line at a time, even when your eye only concentrates on the center of each line.

Of course, not everything you read is going to be two inches in width, with three words to a line. You can, though, use this speed-reading technique by breaking down each line of text into a few "clumps" which you read using the techniques we've discussed — focusing on the center of the clump but taking it all in.

As you look at a line of text, try to identify two or three clumps each made up of three to five words. For each clump, you only need to look at the center. As with the exercises above, you should be able to "take in" the whole clump at once. As you read this way, your eyes will move a bit from side to side, from one clump to another; however, you will only be moving your eyes once or twice from clump to clump, rather than moving to read each word, which will improve your speed.

A good way to isolate "clumps" is by looking for clauses — groups of words that grammatically or logically go together. For example, look at the following sentence:

Before eating breakfast, he went jogging.

This sentence is made up of two distinctive clauses:

before eating breakfast
   and
he went jogging

If you were to speed-read this sentence, each of those clauses could be a clump; for each clump, you can focus your eyes on the central word, but still take in the entire clause. To read the whole line, your eyes can move from the first clump on the left to the clump on the right:

Before eating breakfast,   he went jogging.

If you can't find tidy clauses to use as clumps, any small grouping of three or four words is fine.

Here is an example of an entire passage in which each line is divided into "clumps." Try reading it by moving your eyes from clump to clump, concentrating on only the center word(s) in each. In general, when speed-reading longer lines like this, you still want your eyes to move from top to bottom, concentrating on the center of each line. However, you will have to also move your eyes slightly from side to side as you identify clumps. Try to only move your eyes a few times from side to side in each line; your primary motion should be from top to bottom.

Four score and	seven years ago	our fathers brought forth
on this continent	a new nation	conceived in liberty,
and dedicated	to the proposition	that all men
are created equal.		

Now we are engaged	in a great civil war,	testing whether that nation,
or any nation	so conceived	and so dedicated,
can long endure.	We are met	on a great battlefield
of that war.	We have come	to dedicate a portion
of that field,	as a final resting place	for those who here
gave their lives	that this nation	might live.
It is altogether	fitting and proper	that we should
do this.		

Now try reading the paragraphs below from *The Red Badge of Courage*, finding your own clumps and focusing on the central words in each one:

The Red Badge of Courage

Chapter 1

The cold passed reluctantly from the earth, and the retiring fogs revealed an army stretched out on the hills, resting. As the landscape changed from brown to green, the army awakened, and began to tremble with eagerness at the noise of rumors. It cast its eyes upon the roads, which were growing from long troughs of liquid mud to proper thoroughfares. A river, amber tinted in the shadow of its bands, purled at the army's feet; and at night, when the stream had become of a sorrowful blackness, one could see across it the red, eyelike gleam of hostile camp fires set in the low brows of distant hills.

Once a certain tall soldier developed virtues and went resolutely to wash a shirt. He came flying back from a brook waving his garment bannerlike. He was swelled with a tale he had heard from a reliable friend, who had heard it from a truthful cavalryman, who had heard it from his trustworthy brother, one of the orderlies at division headquarters. He adopted the important air of a herald in red and gold.

How did you do? If it was difficult for you to do this exercise — and it probably was — don't feel discouraged. It takes time and practice to train your eyes to read this way. The more you do it, the easier it will become.

Read word clumps, not individual words. Break each line into a few word clumps and focus on the center of each one; you'll still "take in" the entire clump. Your eyes should only move a few times from left to right each line, as you go from clump to clump. Your main eye movement should be from the top of the page to the bottom.

Practicing Speed-Reading Techniques

The techniques described here probably represent an entirely new way of reading for you. Like anything new, it is going to take a long time to get used to and to get good at doing it. That's why it's important to practice a great deal. Practice these speed-reading techniques on time off from classes and only with readings that are not necessary for schoolwork.

You can choose to adopt some or all of the suggestions listed here. For example, you can minimize distractions and pick up your overall reading pace without necessarily learning how to read in clumps, which many find to be too difficult a skill to pick up. Whatever you find works best for you will be the most helpful.

Reading texts in clumps rather than individual words is the technique that requires the most practice. You can start out, as suggested, with newspapers, as the narrower columns make it easier to isolate clumps and take in entire lines at a time. You might also start out by reading simple, fun books, perhaps those designed for young adult readers.

These books will usually be in larger type, use simple words, and have fewer words per line.

After you get comfortable reading this type of material, select something a bit more challenging. Choose novels or short stories you've read already and are therefore more familiar with. Be sure to start with works with larger print and ample space between words and lines. As you get better at speed-reading, you can move on to smaller type and more complex texts.

Make certain as you practice at home you time yourself so that you can track your progress. Decide on a set number of pages for which you will time yourself, regardless of what material you are reading. Between ten and twenty-five pages is a good standard. A stopwatch will enable you to note minutes and seconds, and make it easy to track your time; however, you can simply use a clock or wristwatch and note your time to the nearest minute. Make certain you write down your start time before you begin. When you are finished with the set number of pages, note your finish time. Your total reading time is your finish time minus your start time.

Of course there are different amounts of words — and different difficulty levels — from one kind of reading to another. If you time yourself while reading different sections of the same source — sections of a novel, for example — you will get a pretty accurate sense of how your speed is improving. In general, though, noting your speed for everything you read should give you a sense of how your general rate is improving.

If you want to be particularly accurate with your reading rate, you can count words. Rather than using a set number of pages as your standard, decide on a set number of minutes (such as five or ten). See how much you can read within that time, noting your starting place and finishing place. Then count the number of words you've read. This is a more tedious, but much more accurate system of measuring your reading rate. You can try doing this every few days rather than every time you read.

In time, you'll find yourself reading faster and feeling more comfortable with these techniques. Only then should you speed-read required texts for classes. Even then, you should only speed-read when it is absolutely necessary because of time constraints. Speed-reading, even if you do it well, is not the same kind of active reading you do using the strategies recommended in previous chapters, in which you take notes and write responses. Speed-reading a text for class is better than not reading it at all; at least you will get a general sense of the overall content. However, you might miss important details and facts that could show up on an exam, and you probably won't retain what you read nearly as well. If you must speed-read a text, try to find time at a later point to read it again carefully, taking notes and writing a response.

Follow Up

The most active way to read — and retain the most from what you read — is to use the techniques we discussed earlier, taking notes and writing responses. When you

Follow up. Take a few minutes to jot down notes, thoughts, and general themes. Reread assignments more carefully and take notes when you have more time.

speed-read, however, you obviously won't take notes at the same time. You can, though, take a few minutes after completing your reading assignment to jot down some ideas. Take five minutes to write whatever pops into your head after having read the text. Note the general themes, summarize the overall content, and list some of the topics discussed. Note your personal response or any questions you had. Write whatever you feel like and however much you can in a brief period; this will help you retain some of what you read.

This exercise is well worth the few minutes; not only does it provide you with some notes for later use, it also gives you some time to reflect on and absorb a bit of what you just read so quickly.

Remember to reread the text more carefully, taking notes and writing a more detailed response, at some point when you have the time. This is especially true of any text you sense is particularly important for the course and likely to lead to questions on an exam.

Index